the story of the *Scottish Daily News*

the story of the

SCOTTISH DAILY NEWS

Ron McKay and Brian Barr

CANONGATE : Edinburgh 1976

*First published in 1976
by Canongate Publishing Ltd, 17 Jeffrey Street, Edinburgh,
Scotland.*

© *1976 Ron McKay & Brian Barr*

*ISBN
Hardback 0 903937 24 7
Paperback 0 903937 25 5*

*Typesetting by Lindsay & Co. Ltd,
Blackfriars Street, Edinburgh.
Printed and bound in Great Britain by Billing & Sons Ltd,
Guildford and London.*

Contents

ERRATUM

p. 111

Julius Springer are publishers of
scientific journals and have no
connection with Axel Springer,
publishers of the "notorious"
Bild Zeitung. The authors
apologise for this error.

Acknowledgments

To David Martin, Jim Russell, Allister Mackie, Charlie Armstrong, Ronnie Gibson, Eric Tough, John Hodgman, Richard Briston, Robert Maxwell, Annette Howat and the others who wish to remain anonymous, but particularly to the 500.

The photographs in the book are taken from the BBC-2 documentary 'The Cost of the *Daily News*'. We are also grateful to the BBC for permission to quote from a number of programmes, and to Granada Television for permission to quote from an edition of 'World in Action'.

Introduction

Two days after the final edition of the *Scottish Daily News* a documentary prepared by BBC Scotland — 'The Cost of the *Daily News*' — was transmitted on BBC 2. The original intention had been to prepare a programme to be broadcast on the first anniversary of the *SDN* launch, but, of course, the paper was to die after only six months and the fifty-minute film went out as a valediction rather than a tribute: Brian Barr was reporter and narrator, Ron McKay provided much of the research.

Some of those connected with the *Scottish Daily News* will question our right to produce this book. And those same people would, no doubt, question our assumption that the paper is dead: at the time of writing a weekly 'emergency' edition is being prepared by those still sitting-in at Albion Street and Robert Maxwell, who is an omnipresent character in this book, is negotiating to produce a Strathclyde evening newspaper from the building.

However, neither of these events justify the conclusion that anything of the *Scottish Daily News* — as Britain's first worker-controlled, mass-circulation daily newspaper — now remains. Most of the principal characters have gone their separate ways — Allister Mackie is selling insurance, Fred Sillitto is a sub-editor on the *Glasgow Herald,* Nathan Goldberg is working on a newspaper for the Third World in London — and even Mr Maxwell admits that his new paper, if it is launched, will be run on conventional lines, with only a gesture towards worker-participation.

We have written our account from two perspectives — that of the involved insider, and the informed outsider. And while we have made considerable efforts to ensure that our version of events is accurate and comprehensive, we have also been concerned to capture some of the flavour of the project in a way which may be interesting to the general reader as well as to those who were, in some way, involved in the project.

Our thanks are due to a number of people, some of whom would prefer not to be publicly identified with our view of events. Several members of the Executive Council gave us the benefit of their information and opinions; David Martin, producer of the BBC Scotland documentary on the SDN gave us considerable practical help and encouragement; Annette Howat transformed our error-strewn journalistic copy into a clean manuscript. Others read the manuscript and offered helpful suggestions, some of which are incorporated.

And our thanks, finally, to Charles Wild of Canongate for his valuable advice and for having the courage to publish when others quailed.

1
Good Friday

March 28, 1975: Albion Street, Glasgow

The late winter sleet came driving down, across the muddy gapsites. It forced the crowd of men and women standing outside the temporary wooden hut to bow their heads and huddle together, but it could not dampen the contagious mood of excitement felt by the hundred or so people who had been standing in the street now for over two hours, staring hypnotically at the steamed-up windows of the hut. Every few minutes some movement into or out of the hut sent ripples of expectation through the crowd and the television crews scrambled for their equipment in case they missed a historic moment.

Rising up behind the crowd, the black glass Beaverbrook building lay cavernous and silent. The building had lain empty for exactly a year, since Beaverbrook Newspapers Limited amputated their Scottish operation in an effort to stem the flood of losses which threatened the whole company. Eighteen hundred highly paid print workers and journalists, engineers and clerks had been thrown out of work by the closure to join the lengthening dole queues in the Glasgow area. Three newspapers had rolled from the twelve giant Goss presses in the building — the *Scottish Daily Express,* the *Scottish Sunday Express* and the *Evening Citizen*; the first two were now printing in Manchester and the evening paper had ceased publication, its name sold to the rival Outram group for £2.75m, giving Sir Hugh Fraser's *Evening Times* a monopoly in the West of Scotland.

Some of the 1,800 former *Express* workers now stood with their families waiting to hear what news the day would bring; others lined the gantry of the Express Bar across the road, drinking to their hopes in a mood of disbelief that this

3

momentous day really had come to pass. For all of them, the desolate black building in Albion Street was the embodiment of their hopes and their dream that they might work there again, but this time as joint owners of the means of production, fellow co-operators in Britain's first worker-controlled newspaper. And they waited, on that anniversary of bitterness, humiliation and defeat, to find out whether the day would bring reality to their dream of a new newspaper — the *Scottish Daily News*.

The one man who could create that reality, Robert Maxwell, millionaire publisher and former Labour Member of Parliament, was inside the hut negotiating with the *Scottish Daily News* Action Committee, a loose group of sixteen men drawn from the trade union leadership of the old Beaverbrook organisation, and with the full-time local officials of the unions. And the news which was seeping out of the hut, pervading the damp spirits outside, was not good. Maxwell was refusing to increase his contribution beyond the promised £100,000, was refusing to meet the crucial shortfall between what the workers had raised and what was necessary to launch the paper, unless everyone in the hut agreed to meet an astonishing set of last-minute conditions which he had imposed.

So the word got about, helped along by Peter the Peddler, seller of rumours, racing tips, razor blades and anything else that would pay for alcohol, that the deadline would pass with the total still several thousand pounds short of the amount necessary. Periodically people pushed through the crowd to deliver last-minute investments. One man, straight off night-shift work, cycled up, his boiler suit stuffed with £1,000 in £5 and £10 notes. But as two o'clock came and went — already four hours past the official deadline for contributions — and the crowd began to drift away to join a mass meeting in the City Halls nearby, there was still £25,000 to find and no sign from inside the hut that Maxwell was prepared to climb down from his demands and provide the money to bridge the gap.

Most of the Action Committee arrived at the campaign head-quarters — a four-roomed wooden hut directly across Albion Street from the *Express* building formerly used as a circulation base — at around eight o'clock on the morning of

4

March 28. The prospectus issued seventeen days previously by Scottish News Enterprises Limited (the company launched by the Action Committee early in their campaign) had set ten o'clock on the morning of March 28 as the deadline by which they would have raised £475,000 in public subscriptions. The workers themselves had paid in £200,000 of their redundancy money from Beaverbrook, Maxwell had promised £100,000, leaving £175,000 to be raised from members of the public in shares of £25 each.

But that day was Good Friday, the banks were closed and would stay closed until the following Tuesday, and the workers were not in a mood, after their long struggle, to be denied by a detail of company law. They were still nearly £40,000 short of the £175,000 that they needed to release a Government loan of £1.2m and to activate an agreement with Beaverbrook to sell the plant and machinery to the co-operative. The Action Committee intended to continue to take in contributions until they either reached the target or were told by the Department of Trade and Industry that they had failed in their objective.

At nine o'clock the sixteen-man Action Committee met to review progress and, in particular, to discuss tactics for dealing with the man they felt confident was going to provide the missing capital, Robert Maxwell. A year before, after Beaverbrook had given notice of the closure of Albion Street but before work stopped, the Action Committee had been formed to fight the closure. When they failed to prevent Beaverbrook's move south, the committee looked around for another proprietor to take over the building and only when that failed was the committee refashioned to spearhead the redundant workers' campaign for a new beginning, a new newspaper for Scotland, and the creation of 500 jobs.

Allister Mackie, a 44-year-old compositor on the *Scottish Daily Express,* was the elected chairman of the committee and its chief spokesman. His credentials for leading the struggle were impeccable, a lifetime's commitment to the labour movement but with an aura of moderation and wholesomeness unlikely to offend big business, whose financial support would be crucial. He had been Imperial Father (convener of shop stewards) under Beaverbrook where his geniality and adroit handling of politically divergent trade unions had impressed the work force, if not the manage-

5

ment. His interest in politics bled over into his private life. He was a Labour town councillor for Bathgate, a mining and industrial town in West Lothian, and his holding of the seat at the last local elections by a whisker-thin four votes against a strong SNP challenge was testimony to his personal popularity rather than his party's. He was a man who sought power but was ill at ease with it, a characteristic that appealed to his supporters. Outside of politics Mackie pursued an interest in Scottish literature and folk-song, being particularly attracted to the writings of Rabbie Burns. There was no deviousness about the man; he was open, warm and interested. You might not agree with him, but he commanded respect.

Mackie chaired the nine o'clock meeting, which was perfunctory and low key. The Action Committee agreed that Maxwell was their only likely benefactor and the more percipient — those who had been closest to the man, like journalist Nathan Goldberg — felt certain that he would meet their cash shortfall, but with conditions. What these conditions were likely to be had been hinted at three weeks earlier. Maxwell had been in Moscow and the committee, worried by the non-appearance of the publisher's promised cheque for £100,000, had instructed their lawyer, Brian Dorman, to telephone him in Russia. Dorman reported back that the cheque would be forthcoming in due course. This reassured the committee, but Dorman had more to tell them. Maxwell, he reported, had a new vision of the *Scottish Daily News,* that of a newspaper providing a rolling diet of news round the clock. His idea was a 24-hour newspaper, a concept unheard of in Britain but already tried, successfully, in other English-speaking countries like Canada, the U.S.A. and Australia. And this 24-hour newspaper was to be produced with the same manning levels as for a morning paper, even though the labour force of 500 was already less than half the size of the staff on most conventional daily newspapers.

The Action Committee, all experienced trade unionists, knew that, however favourably *they* might consider this new suggestion, it would be sharply vetoed by their full-time officials. When the meeting broke up there was unspoken agreement that the Action Committee should accept Maxwell's conditions if only he would agree to invest the missing finance; insuperable obstacles to implementing the conditions could be found after the cash was in the bank. Mackie then left the hut to travel out to Glasgow Airport to meet Maxwell off the London plane.

Long after that day was over, after the *Scottish Daily News* had lived and died, Charlie Armstrong, a former *Evening Citizen* stereotyper, remembered everything he did that day. He remembered the clothes he wore — tightly cut grey suit, brown leather coat — every small act, every gesture, every word, every visitor to the temporary head-quarters. At the time he felt himself part of history; the old was passing, the new was coming in and it all seemed exciting, fitting, memorable. Armstrong was, at twenty-nine, a cocky, aggressive young man — 'gallus' in the Glasgow patois. He had been born in the city's blighted East End and though he now lived in a bachelor flat in a tower block in East Kilbride new town, he still haunted his old stalking ground. It was he who had first met Robert Maxwell in London; the two poor boys from different cultures recognised much of themselves in each other and, perhaps for that reason, had quickly gone through mutual empathy to loathing.

Armstrong recalled that first meeting:

'In the early days of the Action Committee we were phoning up any prominent people we could think of that had any money. We got in touch with Alex McKay, who is number two to Rupert Murdoch on the *Sun*. Nathan Goldberg and me went down to London to see him. We had a bit of spare time and we were lying about the hotel and I remembered that someone on the Action Committee had said that he had spoken to Maxwell. So we said to each other, "Come on and we'll phone him up". So we phoned up and he said, "How long would it take you to get here? I live in Montpellier Square, near Harrods."

'So we jumped into a taxi and went up to 27 Mont-pellier Square, which is a two-storey office-cum-house. We waited a few minutes and were shown upstairs and there was this guy Maxwell sitting behind this imposing desk with half a dozen telephones. He was wearing a midnight-blue mohair suit, a striped shirt and his usual red tie — he must have known we were going to

7

phone that day — and he introduced us to another chap as "one of my solicitors".

'He asked us why we had got in touch with him and we said we had phoned up various millionaires and prominent society people throughout the length of the country. So he immediately set out to impress us — which he did. He asked us how we had got down to London and we told him we had this fighting fund which paid our flights down. So he immediately dug into his back pocket and pulled out a wad of notes and threw them to us saying, "How much have you got there?" I said £80. "There's another £20, make it £100" — all in tenners and £20 notes.

'Then he asked us how much the Albion Street building was worth and we told him Beaverbrook were looking for £2.5m. So he picked up a telephone and said, "Get me Sir Hugh Fraser . . . Hello, Sir Hugh, Robert Maxwell here. I've been speaking to these guys from the *Scottish Daily News*. Now, come on, let's take it away from this boy scout outfit and give it a bit of credibility, give the boys a break. So how much is this building worth . . .?" and, of course, I'm only listening to one side of the conversation, and then Maxwell says ". . . £1.8m . . .".

'Now remember, this is the first time we've spoken to the guy. And then he phoned up one or two other people asking them if they were interested. "One thing you really need is a general manager," he said.

'Were we impressed? No danger! Here he's talking about a general manager and we're running about with the arses out of our trousers. So we said to each other, "Well, we've won a prize." So then Goldberg and I got off our mark and sat among the prostitutes in Piccadilly, in the cold light of day thinking about what had happened.

'At the meeting he'd said the workers had to come up with some of the money, put their money where their mouths were. We told him we'd already agreed to invest a certain amount of money and he committed himself to investing 50p for every £1 we put in; he later changed this to a maximum of £100,000.

'So off we went back to Glasgow. It was terrific; we

8

had this guy, a millionaire, who was prepared to back us. We figured he was interested in political mileage — remember it wasn't long after he'd lost his seat in Buckingham (Maxwell lost Buckingham in 1970 and after disagreement with the constituency Labour Party, lost again in both General Elections in 1974). We thought maybe he was going to try to use this working-class struggle to re-establish himself with the labour movement. What he said, exactly, was, "I'm interested in nothing else except the political mileage."

'Soon after that Maxwell came up to Glasgow and addressed a meeting on the fourth floor of the building where he repeated his phrase about "political mileage" and then he went down to address a mass meeting and they all sang "For he's a jolly good fellow". And that was that.'

Armstrong had been entranced by the man. He returned to Albion Street convinced that Maxwell, who positively reeked success, would infect the enterprise with good luck. Here was a self-made man — with, certainly, a large measure of regard for his creator — who had clawed his way out of the squalor of peasant Czechoslovakia, who had earned himself an impressive war record and who had, through his own shrewd endeavours, built up a multi-million pound business empire. And if he had adopted the mores and impedimenta of the English ruling class — booming upper-class voice, fat cigars and a comfortable life in the soft underbelly of the country — then that was just another reason for believing in his ability to make the enterprise succeed.

If they had nascent doubts about Maxwell's real intentions, the Action Committee suppressed them long enough to hold out a hand to take his cheque.

And now, on March 28, they all waited for Maxwell to arrive as they stumbled through a spaghetti of television cables, answered telephones or wrote receipts for last-minute contributions. A young Glasgow businessman arrived outside the hut — Richard Agnew, part-owner of a chain of cut-price liquor stores. He knocked on the steamed-up window and was eventually escorted into the main room. He told the committee that he wanted to increase his initial investment in the company from £1,000 to £10,000. And the *Scottish*

Daily News was just £25,000 short of its target. It was still only mid-morning and into this chaos of activity and expectation strode the large figure of Robert Maxwell, wearing a camel-hair coat and with cossack hat stuck jauntily to the side of his head. The Action Committee immediately went into caucus with him in the main room, locking out the hullabaloo. He came to the point quickly. He already knew that the co-operative were still £25,000 short and he was prepared to make up the balance, subject to certain conditions. These were that the Action Committee should accept his idea for a 24-hour newspaper, should commit the workforce to working unlimited overtime, and that he should be made publisher of the newspaper and co-chairman of the workers' co-operative. While Maxwell was stipulating his demands before he would make it possible for the project to go ahead, the Fathers of the Chapels (FoCs or chairmen of the various union branches in the firm) were meeting in a separate room. Several members of the Action Committee left the main room to forewarn the FoCs about Maxwell's last-minute conditions. Charlie Armstrong and Nathan Goldberg were the principal speakers, and Armstrong remembers telling the FoCs, 'Just agree to whatever he says until we get his money'. Just before eleven o'clock John Hodgman, chairman of the Glasgow branch of the National Union of Journalists, was wakened by the telephone. A sub-editor on the Scottish *Daily Record,* Hodgman had been working until four o'clock that morning and when he answered the call George Welsh, the journalists' FoC in Albion Street, asked him to come to the hut as soon as possible. Hodgman had worked for the *Scottish Daily Express* for nearly four years, moving to the *Daily Record* six months before the Beaverbrook closure and he had given up a week's holiday to canvass for cash for the *Scottish Daily News,* bringing in several hundred pounds by his own efforts. He knew Welsh as a sub-editor and as a trade union official and had scant respect for him in either capacity.

'Have we made the target?' Hodgman asked.

'No one knows,' said Welsh, 'but there is some problem and Maxwell wants to see the trade union leaders.'

In his capacity as Glasgow branch chairman Hodgman

went to Albion Street, replacing the union's full-time official, George Stone, who was out of town.

It was around twelve noon when Hodgman arrived, making his way through the knot of people and into the crowded hut. He was met in the hall by Welsh and Action Committee members Charlie Armstrong and James Russell, a financial journalist.

'They told me: "Just agree with everything that Maxwell says". I was certainly given the very strong impression that Maxwell was holding up his cheque until he had seen and talked to the branch officials of the unions concerned.'

Action Committee chairman Allister Mackie was in the ante-room adjoining the main room. According to Hodgman, Mackie said to him, 'The man's mad. Just nod your head dumbly and we'll get our newspaper'.

Then Hodgman, and half-a-dozen of the other branch secretaries who had similarly been forewarned of Maxwell's conditions, were summoned into the main room where the great man was holding court. Seated around him at the large wooden table were most of the Action Committee and standing behind them were the leaders of the Albion Street trade unions, the FoCs. Five or six others were running about behind the gathering, grabbing telephones which were going off in ragged sequence. Maxwell called for order.

'I have spoken to the Action Committee,' he announced, 'and they are in agreement with certain proposals that I have made.' He paused to let that sink in. 'I have also spoken to the FoCs about these proposals and they, too, are in agreement.' His gaze swept the circle of full-time officials. He went on: 'I now want you gentlemen to listen very carefully to what I have to say.' From the desk in front of him he picked up a piece of paper. 'This is a cheque — my cheque for £125,000.' There was a burst of applause and cheering and Allister Mackie, standing directly opposite Hodgman, winked.

Maxwell then launched into his plans for the new paper. It would not simply be a morning paper, it was to be 'a totally new concept in British journalism,' an American-style 24-hour paper publishing an edition at tea-time and continuing to update itself throughout the night. This, he said,

11

would best utilise the Albion Street plant and would straddle two markets, ensuring the viability of the project. And it would be done — would *have* to be done — with the proposed workforce of 500. Everyone would have to work unlimited overtime, for which, of course, they would be paid. The Action Committee and the FoCs had already agreed to this in principle, he went on, and he was now asking for the comments of the branch officials.

These officials were, as National Graphical Association representative David Emmerson put it, 'in the hot seat'. But there were soothing interruptions from the *Daily News* men. It went beyond the remit of these officials to make any decision on the plan; their job was to execute the policies of their executives and although each must have known that the final decision would be negative — 'one man's overtime is another man's unemployment,' as engineers' official Alex Ferry put it — they were bound to refer the matter up to their executives for a decision. Maxwell, in typical fashion, had reversed their roles on them, had put them in an employer's position of holding the fate of 500 jobs, of being directly responsible for creating or destroying employment in a contracting industry.

'It was a hellish position to be in,' [said Hodgman] 'to have this sprung on you. To realise that if you said, on behalf of the other members you represented, whose jobs might perhaps be hanging by a thread and who certainly realised that a successful *Scottish Daily News* could end their jobs, that it wasn't on, then you would be writing off the job prospects of the 500. The dilemma was, accept conditions which put the 500 back in work but which undermined the job security of the rest of the industry, or tell these men to their faces that their unions were giving them the thumbs-down.'

It was a decision that could not be taken, either way, by these officials in that crowded room on Good Friday. There would have to be several days of consultation before it could be decided whether the 24-hour *Daily News* was possible. Hodgman spoke:

'The journalists in Glasgow and the West of Scotland welcome the plan to finally launch the workers' co-operative *Scottish Daily News* and will consider your plans for a 24-hour newspaper with great interest.'

Maxwell rose and said:

'Gentlemen, we have a deal — and a newspaper!' There was no disagreement.

The meeting broke up. It was shortly after two o'clock and the Action Committee were already more than half an hour late for a mass meeting of the potential workforce and their families in the City Hall, 200 yards away. As Mackie and Maxwell left the main room, television crews jammed the hallway and Martyn Lewis of ITN's 'News at Ten' approached Mackie for an interview for that evening's bulletin and other journalists closed in looking for a press statement.

'The Press want to talk to us, Bob,' said Mackie.

'Fuck the Press,' replied Maxwell.

'But you're part of the Press now, Mr Maxwell,' Martyn Lewis reminded him.

In a great show of bonhomie the two talked and posed, Maxwell signed his cheque for £125,000 several times and then went out to wave it to the crowd outside. He then led them, pied piper fashion, down Albion Street, still waving the cheque.

The sleet had stopped.

In the City Halls the Action Committee, and Maxwell in particular, took the stage to thunderous applause, hundreds of people on their feet cheering and clapping. Mackie opened:

'Now we have, over this past twelve months, had a long, hard struggle. We've fought against odds that no group of workers in Scotland have ever fought against. We've fought enemies that first identified themselves as friends — it took a while to sift out the friends from the enemies. But we did . . . and we won.' And the rest of his words were swallowed up in a tidal ovation.

But when Maxwell began to speak, those who had not been present at the negotiations in the Action Committee hut soon realised that the signing of the cheque meant nothing until it was actually handed over to the Department of Trade and Industry at a meeting scheduled for three o'clock that afternoon, and until the whole of the workforce had swallowed the three conditions which attached to the money — the acceptance of the 24-hour newspaper in principle, agreement on unlimited overtime and Robert Maxwell as

13

publisher of the *Scottish Daily News*. And, although a few voices were raised in protest at the eleventh-hour conditions, many more voices responded to Maxwell's repeated declaration: 'We have a newspaper, we have a newspaper!'

So there it was — there was to be a *Scottish Daily News* after all, a paper with 'a sense of value and proportion . . . with a philosophy left of centre . . . with the fresh air of freedom blowing through its pages.' But it would also be fettered to Robert Maxwell, his money and his dominant presence.

When the exuberant City Hall meeting broke up the principal characters went off to pass over the cheque to the DTI officials and, thereby, to activate the Government loan to the company of £1.2m, enabling them to buy the building and plant from Beaverbrook. However, a few days later, the Action Committee found out that Maxwell had not provided all of the £25,000 shortfall. Two journalists, Allan Saxton and Ray Chard, had contacted him at his penthouse suite in the Albany Hotel in Glasgow that morning and agreed to put in £11,000 as a short-term loan. In the end, therefore, Maxwell's capital investment in Scottish News Enterprises Limited was £114,000.

At 9.30 on that Good Friday evening a programme went out on BBC Scotland under the title of "Current Account", a weekly current affairs opt-out. Reporters Kenneth Cargill and Brian Barr conducted studio interviews with Allister Mackie, Robert Maxwell and editor Fred Sillitto on one side, and with Allan Gay of Strathclyde University's Chesters Management Centre and David Hutcheson of Glasgow College of Technology on the side of the sceptics; caught in the centre was Professor Richard Briston, also of Strathclyde University, who was then a financial adviser to the co-operative.

After a short historical film on the gestation of the *Scottish Daily News*, the studio discussion opened with Kenneth Cargill asking Robert Maxwell about the source of the £34,000 which plugged the gap in the co-operative's finances. Maxwell, in expansive manner, recounted the story of Richard Agnew's £9,000 cheque. He went on:

'The other £25,000 that was still missing came from me, as an advance against other investments which were still in the pipeline which I will no doubt get reimbursed in due course.'

'Did you lay down any conditions for advancing that money?' asked Cargill.

'None at all,' replied Maxwell, much to Mackie's astonishment.

Maxwell went on to elaborate on his idea for a 24-hour newspaper, one of the eleventh-hour conditions the Action Committee had to accept, and used the opportunity to take a public swipe at Sir Hugh Fraser and his *Evening Times*, 'which, I hope I'm not being too unkind, most of the viewers will agree is rather dull and dreary and uninspiring.' Later in the programme he returned to worry on that same bone:

'Certainly our first edition will compete with the (*Evening*) *Times*, but we don't consider the *Times* competition at all. We're forced to provide a paper because our competitors are so dull.'

The idea behind the 24-hour paper was, of course, to straddle the morning and evening newspaper markets, publishing an evening edition of the newspaper in the greater Glasgow area, with the morning editions circulating throughout Scotland. It was a bold, Maxwellian concept, intended to knock away one of the legs of the argument put up against the viability of the new newspaper by Allan Gay and his team at the Chesters Management Centre. The centre had been commissioned by the Lord Provost of Glasgow, (now Sir) William Gray, to prepare a detailed study of the project and they had concluded that the proposed broadsheet (large size) newspaper was unlikely to capture a circulation of more than 120,000 and it would not attract a sufficient amount of advertising. In short, they concluded, the *Scottish Daily News* was not a viable project.

By pitching the 24-hour paper idea into the debate Maxwell hoped to unsettle his opponents and he succeeded, to a degree. Moreover, although within ten days the print trade unions had soundly vetoed the whole notion, the idea made a considerable impression on rival newspaper managements who now saw a *Daily News,* with the flamboyant Maxwell aboard, as a real threat to their circulation figures. All of the Scottish national dailies — the *Scotsman* and the *Glasgow Herald*, the *Daily Express* and the *Daily Record* — mounted expensive publicity campaigns to try to keep the

15

Daily News at bay. Such a concerted effort to attract readers had not been seen in Scotland for decades; it happened again within six months, when the same newspapers were clawing at the corpse of the *Scottish Daily News*.

But carried along by the brilliance of his own strategy, Maxwell played a dominant role in the television programme, interrupting colleagues and rivals alike, and refusing even to contemplate the possibility that the trade unions might not be too happy with his great idea.

Professor Briston, by now having serious doubts about the growing Maxwell involvement in the newspaper, kept his head down. Only David Hutcheson, a lecturer in communications studies, held his tack on the newspaper's bleak commercial future in face of Maxwell's onslaught:

'I think one must remain sceptical,' he said. 'It's scepticism about the availability of advertising revenue because, whether we like it or not — and I for one don't like it — in this country newspapers depend for their survival on advertising . . . and I'm not convinced that the necessary advertising is actually available in Scotland.'

After the taping of the programme ended, the participants had to wait while technicians completed spot-checks on the recorded programme. While this was going on they chatted casually and Maxwell was asked if the *Scottish Daily News* would be competing in the 'tits and bums' market with the *Sun* and the *Daily Record* (IPC's equivalent of the *Daily Mirror* in Scotland). 'I think we know where to draw the line,' said Maxwell righteously. 'We're a family newspaper, and we will draw the line at erect nipples.' The line, when it was eventually drawn, came below, or perhaps before, bared nipples, not out of any Calvinistic prudery but simply because such pictures cost a great deal more than the unexciting substitute which the *Daily News* slapped on page 3 — dated pictures of well-covered bathing beauties snapped on Miami or Bondi beach in poses reminiscent of the Ladies' League of Health and Beauty.

But the last thirty seconds of the 'Current Account' programme pointed up the direction in which the *Scottish Daily News* was really heading.

Asked if he was looking forward to the next six months, Allister Mackie said:

'Oh, absolutely. Certainly I hope they'll be less exciting

16

than the last twelve months. But if I can make one very quick point: in case Bob himself thinks that he's going to run the newspaper, then he's in for a disappointment. He's part of a team.'

Hairline cracks were already starting to appear in the public facade which would result, almost six months to the day after the paper's launch, in the collapse of the workers' dream amid bitter recrimination.

2
The Closure

The end of the story of the Big Idea was scripted by a wealthy young publishing entrepreneur and carried out with a chilling efficiency that would have horrified the man who thought, up the idea in the first place — the late Lord Beaverbrook. The Beaver's Big Idea for an autonomous *Scottish Daily Express*, was to be 'the greatest landmark in the history of journalism as far as I am concerned. . . . For I have always carried about within my heart the dream that as my father went out of Scotland to speak to Canadians, so I might return from Canada with a word for Scotland.' He wrote these words for the front page of the first *Scottish Daily Express* in 1929, under the headline 'The Story of a Big Idea', and a framed copy of that first paper hung over the editor's chair in Albion Street for clearly fifty years.

Jocelyn Stevens is not a man much concerned with romance and legend. He believes in industrial virility. And the ailing Beaverbrook empire, which he had been brought in to revive, was being bled, he believed, by its northernmost outpost. Beaverbrook's operation in Scotland had been bedevilled by labour-management confrontation — fifty-six interruptions to production in fifty-two weeks — and had never been profitable even in the heady days of the late 1950s when the paper sold 660,000 copies a day. Now, at a time of steepening wage and newsprint bills, the whole empire was in imminent danger of collapse and could no longer sustain the annual £1m drain out of Scotland.

In his approach to management problems and industrial relations Stevens was the elemental man. He believed in straight lines, pragmatic solutions. Never mind traditions or grand conceptions, attend only to the details.

He was a man of endless ambitions who did not dream small dreams or pursue small challenges. And his appetite for achievements was never satisfied. His publishing career thus far had taken him through the foothills to a worthy challenge, saving a great newspaper.

Stevens' first excursion into publishing had been with *Queen* magazine, an ailing publication which he bought in 1957 as a twenty-fifth birthday present for himself. It cost him £250,000 but he had been left three times that amount at the age of thirteen by his grandfather, Sir Edward Hulton. He took over *Queen*, which had become locked in a time-warp of toothy, slightly impoverished gentility, and began to remodel it into a glossy, good-life monthly overflowing with vacuously attractive models, flabby society people and exquisite ephemera. It became a young and bitchy *Vogue* and Stevens perfectly caught the mood of the bred-affluent, people like himself, who envied the hubris of Swinging London but turned up their noses at its vulgarity. His policy was to spend to succeed and never to underestimate the capacity of the consumer to devour.

In 1968 Jocelyn, the fourth generation of his family in publishing, sold *Queen* for £200,000 to Oxley Industries. History caught up with him when he was offered the managing directorship of the London *Evening Standard*, a newspaper his grandfather had sold to Lord Beaverbrook in 1923. He was attracted to the enormity of the problem presented by the *Standard*, the second and less successful London evening, and by the historical inevitability of the situation; it was, after all, a problem for the family.

Putting his up-market philosophy into the mass-circulation *Standard* required a measure of subtlety unnecessary in *Queen*. He had the paper redesigned, pushed a commitment to 'in-depth' coverage and succeeded in reporting at length about very little. But Stevens' perception of the mass mind was acute. He identified that characteristic common in society, exclusive or plebian, the class ethic . . . and he homed in upon it. The *Standard* was ego-based, flattering the reader, presenting a continuity from first page to last, underlining that 'you are what you have', focusing on the bright things, all presented decorously, but artily. *Standard* readers were young, acquisitive, ambitious and on their way. And if the reality was a tedious clerical job and a shabby shared flat, never mind, the *Standard* would flatter your self-conceit.

And, of course, this adman psychology worked. The *Standard* began to overhaul the *News* in circulation and race ahead in advertising column inches. By 1972 Stevens was ready to take on something new. He was made deputy chairman and managing director of Beaverbrook Newspapers, charged by Sir Max Aitken with revitalising the failing *Daily Express* and restoring its profits. Stevens defined his role as being 'The ambassador to the Court of St Max'. Sir Max Aitken, the heir to Lord Beaverbrook's empire, was better known by the nickname Biggles (because of his boyish enthusiasm for aeroplanes and power boats). From the moment he took over the controls Stevens worked according to the formula which had already brought him success in two different markets. He unveiled his formula in March 1973 — calling in DX80 — the *Daily Express* for the 1980s. The paper was to be moved gradually away from its popular image to attract more prosperous readers and advertising. Regional autonomy had to be sacrificed so that the product would look the same wherever it was purchased. This ran directly against the policy of devolved decision-making which had helped increase the circulation of the Scottish paper at a time when the London parent was declining.

The Scottish staff became acquainted with the Stevens formula through a costly internal publicity campaign, with expensive lunches in posh hotels, films of DX80 featuring actor John Alderton, trendy tunes and jingles, all heralding the arrival of the new paper which was going to take Beaverbrook successfully into the eighties.

'The whole performance was ludicrous,' one journalist recalled. 'Technical print experts were sent up from London and spent two weeks at the Central Hotel and eighteen hours a day in the *Daily Express* building just to say there would no longer be ruled lines between the columns.'

Running alongside this formula, which left the Scottish staff mightily unimpressed, was Beaverbrook's legendary voluntary redundancy scheme. This scheme appalled Stevens when he arrived at the *Express*. It had become the music-hall joke of Fleet Street. From a management point of view the voluntary redundancy and early retirement scheme had been intended to shake out the over-staffing throughout the organisation by offering attractive terms for *voluntary* redundancy, since Beaverbrook knew the print unions would resist any measure of compulsion. The scheme was so elaborate that every member of staff was given an explanatory booklet but, in its essence, the idea was to trim 20% of the staff.

From February 1972 until December 1973 any staff member could give notice of his intention to leave the *Express* at any future date during that period. This notice had to be given to management by April 1972. The *Scottish Daily Express* was grossly overstaffed: 1,450 people were paid to produce it compared with the 500 who would produce the comparable *Scottish Daily News*. The long-term plan, therefore, was to clear out the 'dead wood', particularly non-productive staff holding senior positions. On the editorial floor in Albion Street there was a superfluity of under-employed journalists, many of them entrenched in fairly senior positions. But at the crucial point of this plan to trim dead wood and allow new growth, Beaverbrook made a desperate mistake. Instead of offering handsome payments and attractive pensions to those over, say, forty-five and offering little incentive to younger staff to leave, they did just the opposite. They offered poor retirement conditions and, comparatively, very little money to the older people, while making the terms for newer recruits almost irresistible. The company offered a minimum payment, irrespective of service, of six months' pay tax free. So younger people who were sure of employment elsewhere and who might only have worked for the *Express* for a matter of months, could give notice knowing that they would walk out with at least £2,000.

Out of twenty-four sub-editors in Albion Street, seventeen left. And, since down-the-table subs (rank-and-file sub-editors) are a key ingredient in any newspaper, they had to be replaced as they left. Nineteen new sub-editors were taken on to replace the seventeen who left. Altogether forty-one journalists left with bulging pockets to be replaced by forty-three others.

By May 1973, two months after Stevens had unveiled DX80, twenty journalists who had given notice that they were leaving were still working in Albion Street. John Hodgman was Father of the NUJ Chapel at the *Scottish Daily Express* at the time:

'Stevens arrived in September 1972 and just couldn't believe the redundancy scheme. He put up with it for six months and then said that everyone who wanted to leave the organisation had better get out by the following week. But they all had contracts saying that they could work until the end of the year, guaranteeing their wages in the meantime. Some of them just acted like idiots, going around pissed out of their minds every night. Some of them started businesses and ran them from Albion Street to see if they would take off before they left.

'When it got to about May or June Stevens called us all to London, all the FoCs, and told us Beaverbrook were the laughing stock of Fleet Street. "These people have got to go out the door immediately." We told him there was no way. How could they make them leave when they all had contracts. "Offer them more money," he said. "Find out how much they want."

'So I went back to Glasgow and called a meeting of those who were due to leave and said, "All right, lads, how much do you want?" One man was due £4,300. He said £7,000. I got him £6,100. So that was £1,800 extra to leave six months earlier.'

If DX80 was supposed to be the beginning of the beginning, as Stevens termed it, it was the beginning of the end for Glasgow. The managing director was coming to the conclusion that the production of three newspapers from Albion Street and the seemingly insuperable union problems there were more than the Beaverbrook bank balance could stand.

Stevens, and the best and brightest of his management team, planned the closure—which they estimated would cut £3m annually from the debit—in a corner office on the third floor of the Beaverbrook building in Fleet Street. Afterwards he said:

'Although it was a bloodstained issue, the only satisfying aspect of the closure of our Glasgow office was that it was executed enormously efficiently. We worked on it, very few of us, in this room at night after we had done our day's work and every single detail was

22

foreseen and planned. Nothing happened in the fortnight between the announcement and the moment it closed that we hadn't foreseen, despite the fact that we were dealing with a very wild political situation.'

These words became almost a legend for the *Daily News* workers in their thirteen-month struggle to recreate their jobs. They were set in type and copies made to remind the workers of the callousness of management and to spur them on to become their own bosses.

Stevens has a liking for gory figures of speech. He is the clinician 'cutting swathes through' Beaverbrook. He believes that 'people who are not fully employed or past their best should go if the rest are going to survive.' His favourite metaphor on industrial relations is that of a bull fight, with the trade unions, head down and charging, cast as the bull. One year, almost to the day, after brandishing it, Stevens came out from behind his DX80 cape and plunged the sword home. Albion Street closed down and 1,850 men and women lost their jobs.

Denny Macgee claimed that he would be the man who would close the *Scottish Daily Express*. Through his ten years as union leader of the 230 *Daily* and *Sunday Express* journalists Macgee's publicly sworn oath was to slaughter the Beaverbrook knight. Yet his appearance was distinctly unlike a dragon. A wiry, middle-aged man with a shock of swept-back grey hair, he paced the editorial floor purposefully, talked didactically, gestured dramatically. He was the stage trade unionist, given to stabbing home points with his finger and pulling off his glasses in emphasis, allowing them to drop to his chest where they hung by a neck-chain. His mannerisms and booming oratory owed much to his apprenticeship as a vaudevillian. He had played the music halls in his youth but now his performances were restricted to an audience of journalists and managers in Albion Street.

His place in the pantheon of trade union press militants had been assured by his leadership of the first strike by journalists over editorial content — the kind of action which brings out management cries of 'censorship'. The offending matter was a political cartoon by Cummings, the veteran right-wing cartoonist whose work was used by the *Scottish*

Daily Express and its English-based parent, three times a week.

Cummings' cartoons always appeared on the leader page and the journalists in Glasgow were in the habit of making up·the page and leaving a hole for the cartoon, which was always the same size. On this occasion the cartoon arrived shortly before copy deadline and, in the normal way, was sent straight down to the caseroom with only a peremptory glance by the art desk. Denny Macgee was in charge of a department of five people whose sole job was to edit and lay out the leader page.

This cartoon went beyond the normal Cummings stridency, portraying Russian leader Brezhnev, dressed as a priest, leading a procession of Soviet military hardware — tanks, armoured cars, MIG jets — from a Czechoslovak aircraft at Belfast airport. Father Brezhnev was bringing 'alms' to the Irish, his hand in the air giving the peace sign, with bemused Prime Minister Heath and Reginald Maudling looking on. The previous day, in Glasgow, there had been fighting in the streets when an Irish solidarity march took place (indeed a *Daily Express* staffman became photographer of the year with a picture of a young tearaway slashing a plainclothes policeman with a razor during this skirmish). At that time there were genuine fears that the Ulster conflict could spill over into the West of Scotland and in the previous week there had been no fewer than sixty-nine bomb calls threatening to blow up the *Express* building. They had become so commonplace that they were all automatically treated as hoaxes, but as a precaution two of the three entrances to the building had been closed and there was tight security on the third. Against that background, Macgee — himself a Catholic, and the trade union leader with a responsibility for the well-being of his members — felt the cartoon was not only offensive but highly inflammatory, and could be just the thing to incite the genuine bomber. It also confirmed the degree to which Beaverbrook's London base was out of touch with events in Scotland.

After sounding out the feeling on the editorial floor in a number of informal meetings, Macgee stormed off to the caseroom and the other production departments to inform them of the revolt that was simmering on the third floor. When he returned, with the first edition of the next day's paper ready to roll, he called an emergency union meeting of the night-shift journalists. The meeting sent out a demand to editor Clive Sandground that the unions in the building should be given space alongside the cartoon in order to dissociate themselves publicly from it. While the chapel (union branch) stayed in session the editor was asked to make the change. He refused. The chapel then voted, by twenty-nine votes to one abstention, not to allow the paper to go out. By now, however, there was nothing the journalists could do themselves to stop the paper since all the pages had long since been set in type and the presses were ready to roll. The journalists would have to enlist the support of another trade union with the power to stop the presses. The obvious choice was the engineers. Although it is not a print union the AUEW (Amalgamated Union of Engineering Workers) is responsible for maintaining the presses and for setting them in motion. They had already expressed support for the journalists' position on the cartoon and they agreed to use their muscle to implement the journalists' decision.

Later in the night, after the first edition of the *Scottish Daily Express* had failed to appear, the journalists voted again on whether to allow the paper to go out without their statement. The original decision was confirmed by twenty-seven votes to two against. Later still the vote slipped to 24-5 with a noticeable erosion taking place as the management boiled up over the issue of censorship. Shortly after midnight the engineers, who had become the instrument of NUJ policy, went home.

The first stoppage of a newspaper in Britain by journalists in protest against content sent shockwaves throughout the print industry. The next day the full journalists' chapel met and the previous night's decision was retrospectively reversed by 119 to seventeen and the decision to stop the paper was 'deplored'. Editorials in newspapers and trade magazines throughout the country quaked for the future of democracy following this 'blatant censorship' by a small group of journalists in Glasgow. That small group of production journalists — the sub-editors — who by the very nature of their jobs are the most involved politically, the most bored by the long watches of the night, and the most militant, became known in Albion Street as the 'Midnight

Mafia'. And the name of the *padrone*, Denny Macgee, went ricocheting throughout the industry.

Sandwiched uncomfortably between the warring unions and management were the editorial executives, the editors of the three newspapers and their heads of departments. These men saw themselves as the inheritors of the Big Idea and the character they stamped on their newspapers reflected the grandeur with which they viewed their charges and themselves. They went in for big headlines, big pictures, big coverage. Teams of reporters and photographers scoured the ocean in hired planes searching for a stricken trawler; highly paid men fought with their colleagues from other newspapers to snatch an exclusive picture of a murderer being led out of court; pages were gutted and remade through the night when a new story broke. And they specialised in tragedy.

Reporters buzzed around the city collecting pictures of the dead from mantelpieces before the corpses were cold. On the night after the Ibrox disaster in 1971, when sixty-six people died on Stairway 13 of Ibrox stadium at the end of a Rangers-Celtic match, the *Scottish Daily Express* reached a new peak of diligence when it carried on its front page pictures of every one of the dead. How much personal grief was trampled underfoot by *Express* men that day was not recorded.

The style was brash, sensational and simplistic; but it was successful. The *Daily Express* became the biggest-selling newspaper Scotland has known. But from its peak circulation of 660,000 the *Scottish Daily Express* had fallen by early 1974 to 570,000, and more painful than the fall in circulation was the fact that the *Express* had been overtaken by its arch-rival, IPC's *Daily Record*.

The strikes which plagued the *Daily Express* were strangely absent from the *Scottish Sunday Express;* strangely, because the weekly staff were members of the same union chapels as their daily brethren and the industrial relations field was no less furrowed. There were two main reasons for the reluctance of union officials to interfere with the production of the *Sunday Express*: the Sunday paper provided an extra, highly remunerative shift for the daily men, particularly the NUJ officials, and the editorial management of the *Sunday Express* had acquired a

26

reputation for stubbornness in the face of trade union militancy. There were, of course, management-union disputes, but they usually came to a head when the *Daily Express* inherited them a few days later and the presses stopped. In ten years Denny Macgee had never stopped the *Sunday Express*, had never held a disruptive chapel meeting on *Sunday Express* time, yet many of the acrimonious disputes and the longest mandatory chapel meetings in Albion Street were over issues involving the Sunday paper.

One of the most celebrated affairs inherited by the *Scottish Daily Express* concerned a *Sunday Express* reporter who was sacked for incompetence, bringing down the full, if belated, wrath of the daily paper chapel. The Glasgow chapel insisted that the Edinburgh-based reporter could not be sacked. The management's response was to give the man £4,000 and say he was sacked. The reporter managed to arrange that he got the £4,000 and was allowed to resign. The chapel replied that he would not be allowed to resign. So, on March 18, 1971, the chapel went into emergency session over the issue. At seven o'clock that evening the management told the journalists that, unless production started immediately, they would all be deemed to be in breach of contract and would be sacked. By 7.30 they were.

The journalists transferred their meeting to the car park opposite and finally adjourned to nearby pubs when the March winds took the edge off the rhetoric. Twelve executives — earning the name the 'Dirty Dozen' — went back into the building and produced the paper successfully without their colleagues. The issue was resolved the next day with the re-employment of the journalists, with the exception of the enriched Edinburgh reporter.

Sometimes there were on-the-spot protests. The most flamboyant concerned a middle-aged man taken on to do a casual shift as a 'copy boy' and the autocratic editor of the *Sunday Express*, Archie Freedman. The casual's job was to pick up copy from the news desk, the chief sub-editor or the editorial back-bench and send it down the suction tube to the caseroom. Being addressed by the traditional 'boy' particularly irked this man and his gathering rage exploded when he propelled Freedman through a glass partition with a straight right to the jaw. When the man was convicted of assault, the Sheriff remarked on the unusual terminological practices in newspapers which would bring a race relations conviction if used towards blacks.

The last few tempestuous years of the *Daily Express* in Scotland mirrored its beginnings. The paper which had seen six editors in its first four years saw three in its last four. The man who put the paper to bed for perpetuity was a former foreign editor of the London *Express*, Ian Brodie. He succeeded Clive Sandground, a bearded urbane man with a passion for vintage cars and checked tweed suits. Sandground, in turn, had taken over from Ian MacColl who had taken his Presbyterian talents to Fleet Street as (briefly) editor of the *Daily Express*. Following a vote of no-confidence from the journalists in Albion Street, Sandground had resigned, bought a boat which he named the 'Golden Handshake' (he had received £20,000) and went on to become editor of the *Sunday Mail*, the sister paper of the *Daily Record*.

Ian Brodie, a rising young star in the Beaverbrook firmament, took over the hot seat. He was thirty-six and had given up jet-lagging around the world for various publications, including *Newsweek*, to take on plum foreign assignments for the *Daily Express*. He was rapidly promoted through the America desk to the Far East until he took charge, from London, of all the airlifts of foot soldiers the paper was prone to assign to the world's trouble spots. Brodie had caught the eye of Jocelyn Stevens, then still running the *Evening Standard*, when he, virtually alone of all the editorial executives, cried out against the *Express* running the Martin Bormann story — a piece of nonsense about Hitler's deputy being alive and well and living in Argentina. The reputation of the *Express* took a sharp knock, but Brodie's reputation rose in proportion and when Stevens hatched DX80 he asked the foreign editor to pack his bags once more, this time to take on the hostile natives of Albion Street.

Brodie, a tall, thin and angular man who peered from thick lenses, was perceptive enough to realise that Scottish editorial autonomy had to be re-established —at least in the day-to-day news field, if not in the rest of the paper—if the rapid decline in circulation was to be halted. But his baling efforts were rendered futile by the actions of the Midnight

Mafia, and by the end of 1973 the situation was irretrievable; Jocelyn Stevens had started to plot the closure.

On March 18, 1974, after three months of speculation and three days of 'urgent discussions', the board of Beaverbrook Newspapers Limited announced that Albion Street would close. Drastic economies were necessary, they said, in order to save the entire group which, without the closure of Scotland, would collapse within six months with the loss of the remaining 8,000 jobs in the organisation. Beaverbrook, said the statement, had made a loss of £264,413 in the six months to December 1973, compared with a profit of nearly £700,000 in the previous six months. The company's troubles were reflected in the stock market where its shares stood at 37p against 133p a year earlier.

The following day the axeman arrived in Albion Street to take charge of the carefully planned operation. Stevens laid the bulk of the blame for the loss of 1,800 jobs squarely at the door of the unions.

'Exactly a year ago we launched, nationally, a project DX80 to revitalise the *Daily Express* and take it into the eighties. Since that time we have had fifty-six interruptions in normal working in Scotland, forty of which involved loss of sales. This is in one full year, a year of great importance to the paper. So there is a union responsibility.

'We have continuously attempted to motivate and inspire co-operation with our unions in Glasgow and they have been continuously informed of our financial situation. We have received very, very little understanding. The unions now all say "If only you had told us," but how much more could we have told them? The facts have all come home and now they want to have talks on reductions of staff. It is too late.'

Stevens went on to confirm that the closure would be effective in fourteen days and that the title of the Glasgow *Evening Citizen*, published daily for 110 years, would be sold to Sir Hugh Fraser. The closure would cost Beaverbrook over £5m in redundancy payments but this would be offset by Government grants and by an annual saving to the company of over £1m through the closure of the Glasgow centre. The two surviving titles, the *Scottish Daily Express* and the

Scottish Sunday Express, would be printed from Manchester, retaining an editor and up to sixty journalists of the 312 then employed.

On the eve of the closure, when it was evident throughout the organisation that there were to be substantial redundancies in Glasgow, the print unions asked the Beaverbrook management to initiate a tripartite meeting with Sir Hugh Fraser to discuss the possibility of him buying over the Albion Street plant for his own *Glasgow Herald* and *Evening Times*, and printing the two *Expresses* under contract. Two days after the closure Fraser told union leaders that he had found it would be technically impossible to print four newspapers from Albion Street.

As the meeting broke up and the trade union leaders prepared to fly to London to meet Prime Minister Harold Wilson and Trade Secretary Peter Shore, Jocelyn Stevens told a press conference that, ten days before the closure was announced, Beaverbrook's bankers had told the company that they would not lend any more money. 'Between January and March the Beaverbrook fortunes took a turn for the worse,' he said. The problem was a heavy and growing trading loss combined with a desperate shortage of cash — 'the most dangerous combination for modern business'. Stevens said that in January he had approached Sir Hugh Fraser to ask whether he was interested in buying the title of the *Evening Citizen*, which he had now done, but the sudden and unforeseen cash crisis and the banks unwillingness to extend further credit had forced the company to make further economies. It was financially impossible, Stevens added, for Beaverbrook to keep Albion Street open long enough for a possible rescue operation to be mounted.

Sir Max Aitken, chairman of Beaverbrook, confirmed the severity of the liquidity crisis: 'We can't be pushed around any more or we will have to shut the whole thing down,' he said as he emerged from a two-hour meeting on March 21 with Peter Shore. Asked if he would consider a Government loan or subsidy, he replied, 'We will look at anything. But if it is a loan it will have to be interest free. We cannot afford to pay interest.'

Earlier that day a Scottish Trade Union Congress delegation, led by General Secretary James Jack and including Lord Provost of Glasgow William Gray, had

30

attended a meeting at 10 Downing Street. They asked the Prime Minister to ensure an extension of the period of notice in view of the 'disastrous' effect the closure of the plant and building and the 1,850 redundancies would have on the already high unemployment rate in West Central Scotland. And in the House of Commons the Prime Minister said that the Government were giving 'urgent consideration' to setting up a Royal Commission on the Press. Edward Taylor, Conservative MP for Glasgow Cathcart, reminded Mr Wilson that the impending Beaverbrook closure required something more urgent than a Royal Commission.

As the public storm of protest grew, the men at the centre of it, the Albion Street employees, had formed a sixteen-man Action Committee drawn from the trades unions in the building. Their first remit was to try to prevent the closure. The committee was led by the Imperial Father of the Federated Chapel, Allister Mackie.

The *Scottish Daily Express*, in what was intended to be its last appearance from Albion Street, carried a front-page declaration by the Action Committee that the sackings would be resisted: 'We pledge to the Scottish people that we will intensify the fight to ensure that this is not the final edition of a home-based *Scottish Daily Express*.' The committee also called on all newspaper workers to protest at the closure by calling a 24-hour strike, a proposal which was rejected by the unions concerned.

However, another idea was germinating in Albion Street. Andrew McCallum, recently appointed father of the journalists' chapel, had realised shortly after the redundancies were announced that there was little likelihood of a reprieve. And as the passing events confirmed his judgment, he put his idea to the Action Committee: the workers should pool the redundancy money they would get from Beaverbrook, buy over the plant and premises and start their own paper. By Wednesday of the final week this was the only possibility left — remote as it seemed — that would keep the employees away from the dole queues. Tam Dalyell, Labour Member of Parliament for West Lothian, received a telephone call at the House of Commons and he was able to tell an adjournment debate on the Beaverbrook closure that the employees intended to buy control of Albion Street.

'We suggest,' he said, 'that there should be some pressure

by the Government on Beaverbrook to live up to their moral, if not legal, obligation and not put hindrances in the way of such an enterprise. They are morally obliged to open their books and internal operations even if they are reluctant to do so for commercial reasons.'

Replying for the Government Eric Deakins, Under-Secretary for Trade, gave an assurance that moves to form a workers' co-operative would be given 'the fullest possible consideration'. He went on to warn the workers that 'it would be a large and possibly risky operation which would need to be thought through very carefully by all concerned.'

Trade Minister Peter Shore confirmed on Thursday what the men already knew, that there would be no salvation. The workers' co-operative changed from being an idea into a course of action. And when Jocelyn Stevens told the Action Committee that a workers' co-operative would have first option to buy the building and plant, the first step on the thirteen-month struggle had been taken. 'We are now extremely, but realistically, optimistic about the future,' said Allister Mackie.

The decision to give the Action Committee first option on Albion Street was no act of philanthropy by Beaverbrook. Ironically, the future of the *Express* organisation rested with the very men they were throwing out. Cutting off a limb, as Stevens put it, would not alone solve the problems of Beaverbrook Newspapers. There had to be a substantial infusion of cash and that could only come from the sale of the building and plant. The sale of the *Evening Citizen* title had brought in £2.75m, but that was not even enough to cover the redundancy payments; the rest would have to come from the sale of the property for the best possible price. And the best price was the only one. Only the proposed workers' co-operative wanted a specially reinforced, custom-built glass and steel mausoleum stuffed with hundreds of tons of mechanical dinosaurs. Beaverbrook were locked into a grotesque paradox: for their long-term survival they had to sell Albion Street; to sell Albion Street they had to pay off the workforce, and to pay off the workforce they had to help to launch a competitor in Scotland which might decimate their sales and advertising income north of the border. The best sequence of events for Beaverbrook would be a sale of Albion

32

Street to the co-operative, followed by a quick collapse of the new newspaper before it could do irreparable damage to *Express* circulation in Scotland. And, as a bonus, Beaverbrook might find a new brightness to their tarnished image by being seen to be generous to a potential rival.

The fourteen-day death rattle of the Scottish-printed *Daily Express* ended late on the night of Friday, March 28, 1974, amid bizarre and emotional scenes in which grown men wept while others jostled editor Ian Brodie and his deputy. Only 3,000 of the normal 570,000 copies were printed because the Action Committee removed a story from the front page and substituted one of their own — a statement to the people of Scotland from the workers of Albion Street. When Ian Brodie tried to remove the story he was physically restrained. The statement read:

> This is the last edition of the *Scottish Daily Express* as 570,000 know it. Taking its place on Sunday is an English version of the once-great newspaper. Printed in Manchester. Run from Manchester.

> The cost has been almost 2,000 jobs in Scotland with all the misery that entails. This committee is determined to right that wrong. To make sure as many jobs as possible are safe. To make sure that our many faithful readers in Scotland are not disappointed.

> To this end the employees hope to start their own newspaper, one that will reflect the interests and thinking of its readers. Already the committee, which represents the employees' interest, has contacted the Government, unions and industry for their support. The reaction has been very encouraging.

> Beaverbrook have offered their employees first option on the building and plant in Albion Street. The Government has promised us every assistance if the new venture is viable. Having been denied the right of expressing the view of the employees until now, we call upon readers to keep faith with us. Give us your ideas and suggestions for a new newspaper.

Because of the trouble during the preparation of the last edition of the *Scottish Daily Express* the management decided not to go ahead with the last edition of the *Evening Citizen* the following day. For a few days there was a token sit-in by a handful of former employees, after which Beaverbrook closed the doors in Albion Street. They remained closed for more than a year.

3
The Thirteen-Month Struggle

'The entire history of the *Scottish Daily News* is founded on the determination of a group of trade union activists to fight against unemployment. Any other consideration is incidental.' Thus Allister Mackie, figurehead of the struggle by the newly redundant newspaper workers to salvage jobs from the chaos of Beaverbrook's peremptory withdrawal from Scotland, views the birth of the first workers' co-operative in the British Press as a protest against unemployment which might have indicated a new path towards industrial democracy.

As an enterprise, co-operative or otherwise, the *Scottish Daily News* patently failed. Judged as a prolonged protest against large-scale redundancies, the efforts of the workers who refused to lie down before commercial inevitability succeeded. But success in these terms is an abstraction for the 500 men and women who created the *Scottish Daily News* and who, having held back the tide of economic logic for almost twenty months, were finally inundated.

Their struggle began, on March 18, 1974, after Beaverbrook had announced that the company was pulling out of Glasgow. The Federated House Chapel — the caucus of twenty-five different trade union chapels in the building — dissolved itself to give way to an eight-man Action Committee to fight the closure. In all, nearly 1,900 jobs would disappear as production of the *Scottish Daily Express* and the *Scottish Sunday Express* was moved to Manchester and the Glasgow *Evening Citizen* ceased publication.

The nature of the Albion Street Federated Chapel was probably unique in the British print industry: the individual unions which constituted it had, over the years, built up a measure of mutual understanding and co-operation unusual in an operation involving skilled and unskilled, white collar and blue collar workers. The usual manifestation of this federated solidarity was in the form of some kind of industrial action against management and so it could be seen, from that perspective, that the unions were co-operating in their own downfall. However, it is fair to say — and crucial to an understanding of the resistance to closure which preceded the birth of the *Scottish Daily News* — that without the effective, if occasionally uneasy, liaison between the various unions the communal will to fight would not have been forged and Beaverbrook would have shut up shop and gone without leaving any lasting trace in the public consciousness.

In the weeks before the company announced that they were amputating their Scottish arm, there was widespread speculation in the industry that Glasgow was in grave danger. The Beaverbrook empire was rocking in a liquidity crisis and it was well known that managing director Jocelyn Stevens was a pragmatist with little time for emotion in business. The company had even had a perfect opportunity to test the potential effectiveness of distribution from Manchester. A demand for a second day's holiday over New Year in Glasgow was rejected by the company, and the workforce intimated their intention to take the holiday anyway. The *Scottish Daily Express* was printed from Manchester and successfully distributed to all the Scottish outlets. So the management had learned that it was feasible to print from Withy Grove in Manchester, but the lessons from that incident were learned by only one side in the industrial skirmishing that characterised Beaverbrook's Scottish plant.

When the closure decision was announced it was greeted with shock and anger by the workforce. They had believed that the management had been exaggerating the financial state of the company — indeed many even believed that the closure announcement was just another exercise in brinkmanship — and it took some time for them to realise that the wolf had actually come and gone. The union leaders, however, had little doubt that the company intended to carry out the closure and, within seventy-two hours, Action Committee representatives met Prime Minister

Wilson to urge him to intervene. But even in those first few hours it was becoming clear that there was little chance either of a change of attitude by Beaverbrook or outside intervention to save the jobs.

The attitude of the national unions to the predicament of their members in Albion Street was ambivalent. On the one hand they opposed the loss of jobs, but on the other they were constrained by a greater evil, since Beaverbrook had made it clear that if 1,900 Glasgow jobs did not go, the whole empire could collapse and eradicate 10,000 jobs.

The Beaverbrook organisation was, at that time, probably alone among major daily newspaper publishers in that it had nothing to fall back on in the event of a crisis in the newspaper market. The *Daily Mirror* had the International Publishing Corporation and, ultimately, the highly profitable Reed International group to cushion declining profitability; *The Times* had Lord Thomson and his widely diversified millions. Beaverbrook, in contrast, were wholly dependent on the sale of their newspapers and national newspapers have long since ceased to be an area in which hard-headed businessmen become involved.

The newspaper industry, like any other, is regulated by the laws of supply and demand. In the halcyon days of the fifties and early sixties, newspapers had been highly profitable and, naturally enough, the unions had extracted their share of the treasures. Wages in national newspapers were unmatched by any other substantial section of the labour market. But as television began to undermine readership and advertising revenue, the press barons had to look for economy measures. Voluntary redundancy schemes were introduced, wage demands were more fiercely resisted, and alternative technology was considered.

Newspapers have been produced by the same methods for more than a hundred years. Copy, provided by journalists, is typeset in lead slugs, screwed into metal frames (formes), an impression is taken in papier-mâché and a metal plate made from this; the final stage is taking an impression from this plate. It is a heavily labour-intensive method and it has been obsolete for more than a decade. The advent of computer typesetting and web-offset printing have made the jobs of most of the trades involved in the newspaper industry redundant. Type can now be set — and is, increasingly, abroad — directly by journalists at a computer keyboard and printed out on paper which is cut up, laid out, photographed and made into a plate. The installation of web-offset presses (such as IPC's modern plant in Glasgow which prints the *Daily Record*) means faster, cheaper production and higher quality.

If the craft unions have not exactly welcomed this revolution in printing methods, there was a growing realisation among national print union leaders that Luddism would only bring a total collapse of the industry. Three national newspapers had died in the last fifteen years — the *News Chronicle,* the *Daily Herald* and the *Daily Sketch* — and the *Sun* was only saved from extinction by publishing whizz-kid Rupert Murdoch and his bared nipples. So the tremors of alarm that were emanating from the black glass *Express* building in Fleet Street were treated seriously by the print unions. They were committed, in theory, to a re-equipment of the industry and the redundancies that would result. The *Daily Express,* they agreed, was in imminent danger of collapse without the closure of Glasgow or some similar major economy. They could not point to accumulated profits in some other area of the Beaverbrook empire and they realised that the stark choice was between 1,900 redundancies in Glasgow or 10,000 nationwide.

This argument was impressed on the Albion Street men in their meetings with national union officials. The Action Committee, faced with a clear determination by the company to go ahead with the closure and no real will from their own trade union leaders to resist, were forced into an agonising reappraisal of their protest tactics. What was the alternative to walking meekly into the dole queues? The answer, a worker-controlled newspaper, emerged at a meeting of the, by now, enlarged Action Committee. There is a dispute about who actually first mentioned the possibility, but there are two strong contenders for the honour — journalist Andrew McCallum and Glasgow Labour MP, Hugh Brown. At first the idea of creating a co-operatively owned newspaper was dismissed as preposterous. Everyone's sights had been set on preventing Beaverbrook from closing down and that had failed; what chance, then, of funding and launching a new newspaper?

Allister Mackie, the former Imperial Father of the

Federated Chapel, and now chairman of the Action Committee, decided to test the temperature of the water in the week before the closure. In a radio interview he released the information that the men were examining the possibility of forming a co-operative to buy over the plant and building with their redundancy money from Beaverbrook. It seemed a ludicrous proposal and it was interpreted by most observers as an implied threat of a work-in along the lines of the struggle by workers at Upper Clyde Shipbuilders in 1971. But a work-in had never really been a possibility; without wire services, credit and distribution facilities the 1,900 workers would have had to sit idle in Albion Street until their resolution froze over.

One listener who did take the men at their word, who saw in the idea of a worker-controlled business a reflection of his own political ideals, was William Wolfe, chairman of the Scottish National Party. He probably also saw an opportunity to make political mileage out of the closure of the English-based plant and, perhaps, to create a daily newspaper sympathetic to the nationalist cause. Wolfe, an accountant and a member of an existing industrial co-operative, approached the Action Committee to volunteer his help in preparing a feasibility study. The Glasgow Beaverbrook management, taken by surprise by this radical new proposal, opened the books to Wolfe and within forty-eight hours he came back to say that with a circulation of 200,000, advertising content of 40% and a workforce of 600, the proposed newspaper could break even. This was a watershed in the struggle, a tangible hope even if qualified by the acceptance of 1,300 lost jobs.

Mackie's radio interview and the coverage of the new proposal which resulted, brought widespread sympathy and support from all shades of the political spectrum and from the public at large. Mackie has since admitted that some members of the Action Committee saw in the proposal an effective vehicle of protest against a society which sees nothing obscene in unemployment, and that these members assessed the chances of actually launching a newspaper as next to nil, but worth trying. The bulk of the committee considered that the co-operative option was the only one left open and that by effort and application they could create jobs for themselves. But the two factions agreed that they were not going to walk away from the struggle.

The composition of the Action Committee at that stage reflected the general political hue of the print trade unions: two Communists, a broad rump of moderates veering towards Nationalist politics, a sprinkling of Labour supporters; only Allister Mackie had any experience of political activism. As a group they were thoroughly naïve in the context of high politics and high finance but, as events turned out, that was probably what saved them; they kept rising and coming back after every body-blow, to the bafflement of sophisticated observers.

Three days before the closure, Beaverbrook agreed to give first option on the purchase of the building and plant to the fledgling co-operative. There were two reasons for this: Beaverbrook did not want to risk fanning further flames of resentment against themselves just at the time when they were attempting to re-enter the Scottish newspaper market from far-off Manchester, and the company were likely to get a better price from the co-operative than from anyone else. There was, literally, no market for what they had to sell — a custom-built container for obsolete machinery. No doubt the chances of the co-operative actually getting started looked miniscule from Beaverbrook's Fleet Street perspective, but there was nothing to be lost, either financially or in public relations terms, by letting them try.

Looked at rationally the idea of taking over Albion Street made no economic sense. It would be expensive to keep up in rates and heating, it was several times too big for the proposed workforce, it would necessarily perpetuate an outdated production method. Any proprietor coming into the newspaper business for the first time would opt for a highly mechanised print system. But for the co-operative this would have meant a substantial retraining of production staff and even more redundancies. So that was not an option. And at this point, it must be said, the journalists, who later came in for criticism by the rest of the workforce for failing to embrace the co-operative ethic, could have abandoned the rest of the workforce and set up their own newspaper, contracting out the printing to an outside firm. This possibility was investigated by the journalists and the costing indicated that they could produce a highly successful

Glasgow evening paper; but the whole idea was abandoned in favour of solidarity with the rest of their unemployed colleagues.

The last night of production of the *Scottish Daily Express* was charged with emotion. A photographer streaked naked through the building and through the adjoining Express Bar. There were a number of incidents involving drunkenness and vandalism. But the flashpoint of the night came when the Action Committee were refused a request to put their feelings on the closure and their plans for the future in the last edition of the paper. The editor was jostled and a limited number of pirate copies were printed with their statement prominent on the front page. This provoked the London management into withdrawing their offer of first option on the building, which brought a corresponding show of muscle-flexing by the redundant employees—a proposed occupation to prevent machinery being moved out. In the resulting confrontation both sides agreed to go back to the status quo, no occupation in return for first option.

There was now a flurry of parliamentary activity over the closure and the attempt to set up a co-operative. The critical state of the industry, exemplified by Beaverbrook's contraction, prompted the Government to set up a Royal Commission on the Press. And soundings were taken by Scottish Members of Parliament on whether the Government would put money into any new venture born at Albion Street. The response was cautious. But the Government did agree to examine a feasibility study on the project and this was commissioned jointly by the Department of Trade and Industry and a City of Glasgow working party set up under the Lord Provost. The study was prepared by a team of management consultants from the Chesters Management Centre of Strathclyde University. The findings of this team, led by Allan Gay, are discussed in a subsequent chapter but, in summary, they considered the project was not viable.

By this stage Robert Maxwell, as we have seen, had become involved in the struggle and he had, in turn, recruited Professor Richard Briston, head of the accountancy department at Strathclyde University. Briston is a quietly emphatic man and no one's uncritical supporter. He had first come to Maxwell's notice when he wrote an article in a professional magazine about the DTI report on the Pergamon-Leasco affair. Briston examined a number of conclusions reached by the DTI inspectors and showed that they were, at least in part, inaccurate. Briston was defending ordered thought and truth; Maxwell took it as a defence of himself, and noted Briston's name for an occasion such as this.

From the start, however, Richard Briston had reservations about Maxwell's involvement. He warned the Action Committee that Maxwell might well not invest in the paper, that he could get all the political capital and publicity he wanted without ever having to hand over a cheque; and if he did invest it would not be with the intention of being a passenger, keeping to the background. His warnings went largely unheeded.

Another Maxwell recruit was Michael Cudlipp, nephew of the famous *Daily Mirror* editor, and himself a well-known journalist. Cudlipp's brief was as an adviser, sitting in with the Action Committee to prompt and guide. He arrived with a deep-rooted scepticism but left six weeks later full of respect for the struggle being waged in Glasgow.

Cudlipp and Briston soon realised that the forthcoming report from the Chesters Management Centre was likely to be unfavourable and they took steps to minimise its effects. Briston is a partner in a Glasgow-based firm of chartered accountants, French and Cowan, who were asked to prepare a parallel study. A few days later the Chesters report was completed and passed to the Action Committee.

Broadly its conclusions were that the project was not viable because the newspaper would not attract the necessary circulation or advertising revenue; they also considered that the proposed management structure of the co-operative was mined with contradictions. This suggestion that there might be conflict and disharmony in their co-operative idyll angered the Action Committee. They felt that the Chesters centre were looking back over their shoulders at the industrial havoc under Beaverbrook rather than forward to the Jerusalem they were intent on creating. Conflict and confrontation would be a thing of the past, they thought, because a *Daily News* employee would be both worker and boss. And that was a formula, not for schizophrenia, but for a sane and orderly way of remodelling industrial relations. As for the rest of the report, the Action Committee simply dismissed the Chesters conclusions that readership and advertising revenue would be incapable of sustaining the new newspaper. Hadn't the *Sun,* they said, exposed the short-comings of narrow economic logic in the newspaper industry? Produce the right kind of newspaper and orthodox market research totems would prove as reliable as chicken entrails in predicting the future of the *Scottish Daily News.*

There was no doubt, however, that the unfavourable report would be acutely embarrassing to the struggling co-operators, as well as damaging their credibility in financial circles. Robert Maxwell was singularly well-qualified to assess the impact of unfavourable official reports. He travelled from Oxford to Glasgow to try to persuade the Action Committee that the public release of the report would cripple the company's chances of attracting investment and advertising. He argued that the report was based on false assumptions: since his arrival on the scene the picture had changed dramatically — his association with the project would ensure adequate advertising and, in any case, the manning levels would be lower than the 600 projected by the Action Committee. At a midnight meeting in Glasgow City Chambers with Allan Gay, Lord Provost Gray and members of the Action Committee, Maxwell demanded that the report should be scrapped. It was delayed for thirty-six hours and then, with Maxwell back in Oxford, released publicly by the Action Committee.

Making public the Chesters report was a sensible, if diffi-cult, course for the committee. Had it been suppressed it would undoubtedly have leaked to the Press — several journa-lists already had unofficial copies — and the resulting publicity would have been even more damaging. As it was, they had a chance to redeem part of the lost credibility. Within twenty-four hours the Action Committee released the French and Cowan report which concluded that given a circulation of around 240,000 and a 40% advertising content, the paper would be profitable. The workforce had also carried out their own, unscientific market research, stopping people in the street to ask them if they would buy the *Scottish Daily News* every day for a trial period of three months. More than 150,000 out of 180,000 interviewed had said they would.

This second report became the basis of the company's

43

application for, initially, Government grant aid of £1.75m under the Industry Act.

Meanwhile the Action Committee members were calling on the general secretaries of all the national unions asking for investment. Since the political line of the proposed paper was pledged to be left of centre, and given the co-operative principle that was to be embodied, the men might have expected a better reception than they got. Their case, they felt, was unanswerable: cast out by Beaverbrook they were appealing to the working-class movement for help. With the exception of ASLEF, the rail union, who immediately gave £5,000, the men met an indifferent, and in some cases hostile, response. Various reasons were given, from union rules prohibiting investments which could not be recalled instantaneously, to the involvement of Robert Maxwell in the project. Even those most sympathetic to the appeal said that they could not invest unless, and until, the Government and the print unions had put in money.

By the beginning of June 1974 the Action Committee were staring bleakly at the £250,000 the former employees had put in and facing up to the prospect of defeat. They had, they felt, been let down by the trade union movement, in particular by their own print unions, and by the Government. Following an unfavourable recommendation to the Cabinet from the Industrial Development Unit of the DTI, very much along the lines of the Strathclyde study, it seemed that the Labour administration was sitting out the Albion Street struggle, hoping it would dissipate itself.

But the *Daily News* men had a friend at court in the shape of Tony Benn, the left-wing Industry Secretary. In July, as Benn was on the point of approving, in principle, for a loan of £1.75m to the co-operative, the co-operators were attending a crisis meeting. More and more members were leaving and the investment was gradually draining away. The Action Committee were split on whether to admit defeat — some doggedly optimistic, others arguing that it was now fruitless to go on. There was consensus on one thing, that the whole workforce should be warned that the struggle could not go on for much longer. At the lowest point of that meeting word came through to Allister Mackie that a message was on its way from Tony Benn. Hearts started to race. The sixteen men waited in the wooden hut in Albion Street in nail-biting silence for the telephone to ring. The call, when it came, was from the Glasgow office of the DTI saying that the telex was being sent at that moment from the London office.

The telex began to run and as it did the committee's hopes soared: the Government had decided to ignore their own professional advisers and offer a *loan* to the co-operative. The offer, however, was hedged around with conditions that the euphoric committee men did not begin to appreciate until the message was examined at greater length the next day. The Government was insisting that the company find 50% of its capital from sources who had read and understood the unfavourable DTI report. In addition, the £475,000 that the company claimed had been irrevocably committed had to be turned over in cash: £500,000 in equity and unsecured loans, and £775,000 in loans.

Professor Richard Briston, now the co-operative's most trusted adviser, urged the Action Committee to bargain with Beaverbrook for a reduction in the selling price of Albion Street. Beaverbrook wanted £2.4m but Briston was convinced that they would settle for nearer to the valuation the Action Committee had been given by an assessor, £1.4m. Briston argued that the Beaverbrook organisation could hardly refuse any reasonable offer, such was the depth of their cash crisis, and there was patently no other buyer in sight. After a protracted bout of Indian wrestling Briston was proved correct. The new price was agreed at £1.6m.

Following this major success the co-operative re-assessed its capital requirements to find they now needed £2.4m to launch the paper — £1m less than they had originally budgeted.

Briston had not finished, however. He suggested going to Beaverbrook again, asking *them* to make the secured and unsecured loans demanded by the Government. Some members of the committee thought that he had gone over the brink, that the *Express* group would never lend £725,000 to a rival newspaper. But again he returned from London having successfully judged how far he could go, how necessary the sale of the Glasgow building was to the company. The Beaverbrook organisation had agreed to make an unsecured loan of £500,000 to the co-operative and a £225,000 secured loan.

The investment contribution by the workers themselves

had, by this time, fallen to £225,000. Maxwell, on the basis of his agreement to put in 50p for every pound by the workforce, was committed to £112,500. There was also commitment of £60,000 from the public and the labour movement (including £30,000 from the Upper Clyde Shipbuilders fighting fund). To make up the £475,000 insisted on by the Government, public subscription for £77,000 was required. A more sensible solution seemed to be a bridging loan from the Government, allowing the co-operative to launch the paper and use its columns to canvass for investment in their company, Scottish News Enterprises. The Action Committee were confident that the Government would advance the loan — after all they were paying out more than £20,000 a week in welfare benefits to the Beaverbrook survivors and it would be months before the prospectus for public subscription could be completed. It seemed only economic sense that the Government would accede.

A few days later, back came the reply: the capital would have to be raised in full before the launch of the paper. The rallying spirits of the workforce were temporarily dashed until Richard Briston urged the Action Committee to publish the prospectus and be damned. In the event of the public subscription failing to meet the imposed target of £475,000 Beaverbrook, he said, would make up the shortfall. There was almost no limit to where the company could be pushed in their anxiety to sell the building and plant, including the underwriting of the competing newspaper's prospectus.

Robert Maxwell, however, had different ideas. He insisted that Briston's line was too hazardous, that no one would invest in the share issue of a company which was not properly underwritten to start with. Indeed, he doubted if he himself could invest unless the project was underwritten. The pressure of his argument won and the launching of the prospectus, due in December, was put off indefinitely to allow Maxwell and the Action Committee to negotiate with the DTI and Beaverbrook over the underwriting problem.

Briston was put out. His tactic had been to create an irresistible momentum in launching the prospectus, which the Government would find politically impossible to reverse if objection was subsequently found to Beaverbrook underwriting the issue. What he was proposing did not strictly meet the loan conditions but he was arguing that for the sake of an uncrossed 't' the Government could not afford to abort the project.

What he feared, in telling the Government in advance that Beaverbrook might meet the balance should the share issue fail to raise £475,000, was that they would object. And they did. They insisted that the loan conditions be scrupulously fulfilled and that there could be no further back door investment from Beaverbrook. There had to be a declaration of support for the paper from the public in the way of investment. This, the Action Committee thought, was a peculiarly tortuous logic. Investing in a company, with a minimum subscription of £25, and intending to buy the newspaper that company produced, were not necessarily compatible. One could support the paper by buying it daily —and the Action Committee were convinced that more than 150,000 would for at least three months — but be unwilling or unable to put in a cash investment of £25.

The argument cut no ice with the Government and by this time the Action Committee had formed the distinct impression that the Government's offer of a loan was, in reality, only a gesture and they hoped their stringent conditions would prove an insuperable obstacle to the co-operative. And it was doubly frustrating to the co-operators as Beaverbrook had just agreed to underwrite the prospectus up to a limit of £150,000. This was in January 1975, ten months after the Beaverbrook closure. The survivors were facing their first anniversary on the dole and jobs were still, tantalisingly, just out of reach.

The time limit on the Government's loan would expire on April Fool's day. The Action Committee were determined that they should have the fullest issue period possible, urged on them by their lawyers, to give adequate time to raise money from the public and the various organisations which had given paper commitments of financial support. Due to various changes in the prospectus, insisted on by Maxwell, the planned six-week issue had to be telescoped into three to meet the time limit. During the three weeks the workforce canvassed Scotland for contributions: factory gate appeals were held, sports and social clubs visited, shops and offices, schools and hospitals.

On the morning of Friday, March 28, Good Friday, as the ten o'clock deadline passed, the cash position was as follows: the investment from the men stood at £200,000 (shrunk by members' withdrawals), Maxwell had agreed to put in £100,000 on his 50p for a pound principle, £161,000 had been raised from the trade unions and public. The newspaper was, however, still £14,000 short of the target set by the Government.

There was only one possible benefactor in sight.

4
The Doubters

If there was a siege mentality amongst the men and the women of the *Scottish Daily News*, struggling to launch their newspaper, it was understandable. Informed opinion, although often sympathetic to their cause, was almost uniformly sceptical about the viability of their project. But the distinction the co-operators could never quite make was between reasoned doubt on the one hand and malice on the other; anyone voicing an opinion contrary to the flood of optimism which washed out of Albion Street was more than a heretic, he was an enemy out to destroy the employment hopes of 500 brave men and women. And this hysteria and paranoia, perhaps understandable in working people whose livelihoods have been obliterated to meet profit targets, was a constant element throughout the thirteen-month struggle and during the brief life of the paper.

The first 'villain' to reveal himself to the *Daily News* men was Allan Gay of the Chesters Management Centre, a specialist unit of the University of Strathclyde. Gay and his team were commissioned to prepare a report on the feasibility of the proposed *Scottish Daily News* by a working party set up by the then Lord Provost of Glasgow, (now Sir) William Gray. The twenty-one-man working party, which met three times during April and May of 1974, invited the Chesters team to report on the potential market in readers and advertisers for a new popular newspaper in Scotland and to assess the chances of success or failure of the Action Committee's proposals.

When their report was published on May 14, the team concluded that the *Scottish Daily News* could not succeed as a self-sufficient enterprise; and that the paper could not be feasible 'so long as the *Scottish Daily Express* continues to be published'.

Gay and his team used, as a basis for their conclusions, a market survey of 521 adults in Scotland, with a geographical split between East and West consistent with the probable market for the paper. From this survey they concluded that there would be a potential market of between 120,000 and 200,000 readers, substantially below the 250,000 the paper would probably need to be successful. The survey did, however, uncover widespread sympathy for the sacked workers and a belief amongst most of those interviewed that there was a need for a new Scottish newspaper. But it revealed a firm resistance among the public to buying more than one newspaper a day. And any new paper, respondents thought, should have a policy line and presentation similar to the *Scottish Daily Express*. The *Express* had lost only 100,000 readers in Scotland following the move to Manchester, far fewer than most people had predicted.

But if a new paper should, according to the report, look to the *Daily Express* as a model for its political stance (hardly left of centre as the *Daily News* promised to be), it emphatically should *not* copy the *Express's* broadsheet format. People interviewed overwhelmingly wanted a tabloid newspaper — the *Sun* and *Daily Mirror* and *Daily Record* size — which is easier to manage on public transport, where most buyers do their initial reading.

On advertising, too, the report was pessimistic. Chesters reported that, whereas there appeared to be a need for a newspaper with readership characteristics similar to the *Scottish Daily Express,* and catering purely for the Scottish advertising market, it was highly unlikely that it would reach the target of a fifty-fifty balance between advertising and editorial content. And Chesters pointed out that the *Daily News,* with a projected cover price of 6p, would be 1p dearer than its competitors and would not have certified sales figures with which to entice potential advertisers.

Manning levels, too, would have to be reduced, from the planned 604 to 500 and a strong and respected management team of some half-dozen would have to be recruited.

Gay and his team estimated that, if their interpretations of the readership survey were correct, and if the advertising/editorial ratio reached 1:07 (the highest they believed possible) the paper would be losing £14,000 a week, even on the reduced manning. Only with a circulation of 200,000 and a consequent increase in advertising revenue through those additional sales, could the paper begin to move into profit.

The reaction of the struggling workers to the report was fierce. The team were dismissed as 'amateurs' who knew nothing about the newspaper industry; they were accused of having misinterpreted the survey data; and their findings were rejected because they had brought untrustworthy academic (the ultimate slur) criteria to bear in a field where 'feel' and experience, engrained with the printing ink, were the necessary qualifications. Their accusers pointed to the *Sun* and the *Daily Mail* as two examples of newspapers which had defied the laws of economic logic.

'In some cases one felt' [Gay said later] 'that t᾿ e report itself had not been read. There was criticism because the Action Committee expected the report to support them, and when they found that the report was coming out against the project, there was an automatic rejection of it by the committee.

'One was a little annoyed at the suggestions of amateurism, the suggestion that the report was naïve. The survey was carried out by a highly professional body who would have bitterly resented the accusation of amateurism and the interpretation was done by a highly qualified statistician. Then the follow-up work which we did ourselves we think was done in a very professional way.

'Take, for instance, the manning figures given to us by the Action Committee — the so-called professionals. A minimum of 600, they said. We were quite sure the figure was far too high; instead we identified a figure of 500, simply interpreting what might be reasonable loadings. And suddenly, of course, this new figure became the correct manning level.'

In public, Gay remained detached from the furore his report had provoked, although privately he had a good deal of admiration for the fight the redundant workers were putting up for the right to work again in their own trades;

but he had to temper his admiration with realism about their remote chances of success.

'I had to suppress my own emotional wish — to have a Scottish paper to replace what has virtually become a Scottish edition of an English paper. From the point of view of a management study this was going to be a most fascinating experiment with a unique management structure. If we had come forward saying that we genuinely believed that the paper would be a success we would have been in there on the ground floor with a ready-made research laboratory. And I was very impressed with the idea of a committee of the Fathers of the Chapels whose intention was that under no circumstances would production be stopped; at the moment of dispute the agreement would be that they would continue production while they were ironing out the dispute. This would have been a most interesting development in industrial relations in Britain.

'So, from the pure study of an organisation this would have been a great thing to see working. On the other hand we could not encourage people to start on something which, in our view, was going to lead to failure if all they were doing was giving us further experimental work. That would have been immoral in the extreme.'

To some of the Action Committee the role of the national trade unions was immoral in the extreme. While publicly affirming their support for the struggle being waged in Albion Street, the unions who had members involved were contributing little more than rhetoric. Only the workers of the former Upper Clyde Shipbuilders, whose own fight against unemployment made them fraternal comrades of the ex-Beaverbrook men, immediately ploughed in £30,000 from the remnants of their fighting fund.

The Scottish Graphical Association, with over 100 members left in Albion Street, were pledged to contribute £30,000 according to the company prospectus of the *Scottish Daily News*, but in fact the union only contributed £5,000. Why the discrepancy?

Fred Smith, general secretary of the union:

'This (£30,000) was the figure that was being

discussed when the proposal to invest was first made. But after our executive committee had examined the rules and consulted our auditors we found that we couldn't make an investment of that scale. The rules say that any investment over £5,000 has to be invested in particular kinds of funds, but in all cases the recall of the money has to be instantly available. I think this inhibition applies in most unions for the simple reason that the union funds are the ammunition for any dispute.'

And the spectre of Robert Maxwell, a publisher who had been blacklisted by the National Union of Journalists, could never be exorcised from the consciousness of some trade unionists, although they were understandably cautious in expressing their reservations. Fred Smith:

'I think his (Maxwell's) involvement is a very — umm — interesting facet. He is not unknown in the world of print. I find it not easy to reconcile his participation in the ownership of the newspaper with the claim that it is a workers' co-operative.'

Three hundred journalists had been made redundant with the Beaverbrook closure. Yet the National Union of Journalists vacillated about investing in a paper which would provide nearly 100 new jobs. After contributing £500 to the newly redundant workers' fighting fund they seemed to shy away from any investment in the new daily newspaper. And Robert Maxwell's presence seemed to be a major factor in their decision. John Hodgman, chairman of the Glasgow branch of the union, decided to go to the annual delegates' meeting in Cardiff and use grassroots support for the *Scottish Daily News* to press a motion compelling the executive to make some investment. The union was in a poor state, financially — one of the proposals to be debated was a swingeing increase in contributions to meet an alarming deficit — but Hodgman felt that members of the executive were hiding in these dark fiscal shadows, concealing their true position of outright hostility to the *Scottish Daily News* and deep-rooted scepticism about the claim that it would be a workers' co-operative.

'I felt that the union had taken a private decision not to invest because it did not believe in the integrity of the struggle, or the calibre of the people involved. And there was no doubt that the involvement of Maxwell played a big part in that. But publicly the executive was using the union's cash crisis as an excuse to knock back the Albion Street men.'

There was now an added personal incentive for Hodgman to succeed in his mission. He had decided to leave the *Daily Record,* where he was a sub-editor, and move to the *Daily News,* taking a wage cut of £40 a week in the process. Hodgman went to Cardiff under a cloud. He had been largely responsible for a decision by the Glasgow branch to invest £200 in the *Daily News.* He had put the proposal before a normal monthly meeting of his branch and then at a specially convened meeting: the decision to invest was taken and then confirmed without dissension, in the full knowledge that the branch was infringing union rules and that Hodgman, and the other officials, could be held responsible. The constitution of the NUJ does not allow individual branches to make donations or investment but, provoked by what he saw as moral dereliction by the executive, Hodgman decided 'to hell with the union.'

The Cardiff delegates' meeting was in April, after the Albion Street workforce knew they had reached their financial target. Hodgman argued that the executive had been negligent in its concern for the unemployed journalists in Glasgow by refusing to invest in the project. More than 400 delegates listened as Hodgman, a bearded, puffy figure, proposed a composite motion instructing the union to invest £1,000 immediately in the paper, censuring the executive for 'its short-sighted and cowardly attitude', and supporting the Glasgow branch for its illicit donation; the motion also welcomed the co-operative as a 'blueprint for the future takeover of failed newspapers under workers' control.'

'I bring you fraternal greetings from the men and women working in Glasgow to produce a new daily paper,' he said. 'A week ago, almost to the minute, I stood in a meeting (on April 17) at which the workforce decided unanimously to remove the executive authority and title of publisher from Robert Maxwell. It was then that I knew for certain that we were going ahead and setting up a co-operative.

'This £1,000 may well be the best-invested money that

the ADM could put anywhere, in any enterprise. I don't think we can tolerate any argument about whether or not we can afford the money.

'A number of delegates have come up to me and said, "There are a lot of things we don't like about this paper, but we are with you morally." Now we are asking you today for £1,000 so that we can show that the NUJ is behind us.

'Most of you know what choice the Glasgow workers were faced with. We have got 500 jobs where there were no jobs at all, to produce one paper where there were 1,800 jobs to produce three. We have set up a structure that ensures that a ten-man board will always have six members from the shop floor.

'The NEC has been short-sighted and cowardly. They were short-sighted enough not to invest in the project and they never realised what the feelings about it at this ADM were going to be. They set up a complaints committee to investigate the Glasgow branch, because we did invest in it. When we discussed this investment at branch meetings the decision was unanimous every time, except for one abstention on one occasion. If people want to challenge the branch, let them challenge it. If you want to haul us over the coals, do that. But that £200 belongs to the *Scottish Daily News* and there is no way that money is going back.'

Hodgman sat down to a rousing ovation and was followed by Bill McAllister of the Highland branch of the union who hammered home the message that the union would be 'morally bankrupt' if it did not invest.

Kenneth Morgan, general secretary of the union, defended the executive, citing the fragile financial state of the union and pressing on the inflamed issue of Robert Maxwell.

'Look at the background,' he declared. 'The company has put out a prospectus which had to carry a Government warning — like on cigarette packets — that this was not an investment to be recommended.

'Look at the structure and personnel involved. The major individual shareholder in this enterprise is publisher Robert Maxwell, who was on this union's warning list over ten years ago. I am glad to say that we were able, ultimately, to withdraw our recommendation to members that they should not work for the publications of this gentleman, but it is not a pattern I particularly want to see repeated.

'The principal preferential shareholder, who has a right to repayment of any capital of his at risk before any ordinary shareholders or trade unionists can come into it, who has the power to convert their loan into shares, is the very management (Beaverbrook) which closed down the *Scottish Daily Express.*'

Morgan's salutary message was lost in the fever among delegates to stand behind the *Scottish Daily News*. The conference agreed to invest £1,000 and concurred with the Glasgow branch decision to invest £200. But it struck out the clause critical of the executive and did not accept that the paper could be a model for workers' control in the industry.

Having established the principle that the NUJ should support the project, Hodgman and his *Daily News* colleagues could afford to be magnanimous. Hodgman telephoned chairman Allister Mackie and told him he proposed to return the cheque he had just won from the union if the executive council agreed. The money made little difference, now, to the paper as it had reached its subscription target and, after all, the NUJ was heavily in the red. Mackie agreed and, honour satisfied, Hodgman told the conference two hours later that the *Scottish Daily News* did not want to add to the union's financial problems and the money would be returned.

'After the *Daily News* folded,' [Hodgman recalled] 'I had a phone call from Ken Morgan. He said, "I never say I told you so, but I told you so." He was right. I don't regret fighting for the money. What I do regret are the assurances I gave to delegates that they had no need to worry about Robert Maxwell. I feel really penitent about that.'

The thirteen-month struggle to produce the *Scottish Daily News* gave the 500 co-operators a new perspective on their trade unions. They felt let down by the national officials, betrayed by their refusal to be swept along by the grandeur of the dream. These officials, it was said, had been stubbornly cynical and if this was true — and the Albion Street workers will not be convinced otherwise — there was one compelling reason for it: the prospect of a successful *Scottish Daily News* brought to life new demons for the unions.

The newspaper industry, in Scotland as well as in Britain as a whole, was facing a steady decline and the creation of a new and unpredictable newspaper would not only undermine established practices but would threaten jobs in other marginal newspapers; it would provide employers with concrete argument for eroding traditional demarcation lines and manning arrangements.

The pool of newspaper readers is evaporating steadily and inexorably. The total circulation of national newspapers had declined by 7.6% in the period 1961-73; in the same period *popular* newspapers declined by 10.9%. The *Scottish Daily News* would be plunging into this diminishing and highly competitive market.

It is estimated that 1,750,000 morning newspapers are bought in Scotland each day. Around 200,000 of these are editions of (British) national dailies. The circulations of the morning papers printed in Scotland, in the period July-December 1973 (the latest figures available during the thirteen-month struggle) were:

(Aberdeen) *Press and Journal*	104,000
(Dundee) *Courier and Advertiser*	126,000
(Edinburgh) *Scotsman*	80,000
(Glasgow) *Daily Record*	589,000
(Glasgow) *Glasgow Herald*	89,000
(Glasgow) *Scottish Daily Express**	571,000

*Now, of course, printed in Manchester.

To succeed, the *Scottish Daily News* would require to win readers away from these papers and, in particular, from the popular newspapers selling in Scotland — the *Daily Record,* the *Daily Express* (which went on to lose 100,000 readers after the move to Manchester), the *Sun* and the *Daily Mail.* Even if the *Daily News* picked up all of the 100,000 readers lost by the *Express* (an unlikely assumption given the difference in politics between the *Express* and the proposed new paper), it would still require to draw at least a further 100,000 from its rivals.

So there was no doubt in anyone's mind that success for

the *Daily News* could only come at the expense of other, or another, newspaper. And the target in sight, from Albion Street, was the *Daily Express*. That newspaper would have to be effectively killed off in Scotland before the *Scottish Daily News* could live. Although the co-operators relished that prospect even though, inevitably, it would mean that other print workers would experience the humiliation and indignity they had so recently known, the trade union hierarchies could not countenance such a reduction in the overall number of jobs.

The other challenge that the *Daily News* presented to the unions was the possibility of erasing, or at least redrawing, traditional inter-union demarcation lines. On this island of industrial democracy such historically sacred institutions were an irrelevance — they were all bosses now; the only constraint on the total disintegration of the union fabric within Albion Street was the awareness that their island was not self-sufficient and that their brother trade unionists still had to survive in the turbulent, commercial ocean.

If there were worries in trade union headquarters about the nature of the new animal being created in Glasgow — and the *Daily News* men would have argued that they were exaggerated — there was also doubt about the calibre of the editorial staff who were to produce the paper. The feeling among other journalists was that those left in Albion Street after the Beaverbrook departure were those who could not get jobs in the industry: as they were functionally unemployable they had to create their own employment. It was said by one senior journalist, that the devotion of the Albion Street journalists to the co-operative ideal was in inverse proportions to their talents.

The truth is that the standard of the reporters and sub-editors was no lower than on rival newspapers (indeed there were several fine talents at Albion Street), it was just that the standard had to be so much higher. Because of the under-staffing, the lack of finance and the dearth of national news and features coverage, there was no room for passengers. And too many of them were too used to the gravy-train years of Beaverbrook to adapt to the hard times of the co-operative.

The *Daily News* might take a left posture, it might

profess itself to be on the side of 'the wronged individual . . . fearless in its views,' but it could never be anti-business or capital. More important to the success of the co-operative than the goodwill and support of the public would be the approval, tacit or otherwise, of big business. Newspaper economics dictate that news — 'the grey stuff between the advertisements,' as Lord Thomson called it — is brought to the reader by courtesy of the advertiser and the entrepreneur. One subsidises the cost of it, the other disseminates and evaluates the usefulness of it. To earn the £3,500 a day necessary to keep the cover price at a realistic level, this newspaper had to convince advertisers that its outlook was not anti-consumer. And it had to prove to businessmen that its politics were not revolutionary if it was to be allowed the licence, through credit, collection and distribution services, to operate in the market place.

William Forgie, deputy managing director of the Fraser newspaper chain, gave his thoughts on the likelihood of the *Daily News* surviving hours before its launch:

'I think the market in Scotland is well covered by other newspapers and the findings of the Chesters team were conclusive, in my opinion, in that they could not get more than a circulation of perhaps 120,000. At which point they would be incurring losses of perhaps a million pounds per annum.

'I do not think they will reach 250,000 circulation and I do not think they have sufficient working capital. And I cannot see the management structure being totally effective.

'This cannot even be called a workers' co-operative newspaper. I think this is another of these myths that have been spread around. This is a newspaper that's owned almost by the taxpayer. The workers have only put in £200,000 out of a capital requirement of £2.4m. So no way can this be called a workers' co-operative newspaper. Beaverbrook too have given a favourable price in the purchase of plant and buildings and given a loan. There is no question about it, this is unfair competition. In this modern climate of helping lame ducks the Government have overlooked one significant point: that is that if this newspaper is successful it could well endanger the jobs of other employees in other newspaper companies.'

The lubricators of the market system are bankers, and these staid and ultra-conservative financiers refused to provide liquidity, either in loan or overdraft, throughout the short, unhappy life of the paper. In July 1974, Jim Russell, the financial journalist, and Denny Macgee, former trade union activist, approached the Bank of Scotland to arrange overdraft facilities to the extent of £1m. They met the bank's joint managing director, Mr David Ferguson, a man who had been part of the Lord Provost's committee which commissioned the Chesters Management feasibility study.

A few days later the firm of French and Cowan, the *SDN's* accountants, received the thumbs-down from the business world in the form of a letter from Ferguson. He said, in part:

'As you know, the bank, right from the outset, has shown a considerable degree of goodwill towards the Action Committee in their efforts to establish a new Scottish daily newspaper. We were actively involved with the original working party . . . and we shared in the feelings of regret which everyone experienced when the feasibility study . . . concluded that the proposition could not succeed as a self-sufficient enterprise.

'. . . and I much regret that we remain in doubt as to the viability of the proposed newspaper. In the circumstances we are sorry but we cannot see our way towards providing the finance requested. . . .'

Adding to the downpour of cold logic falling on Albion Street was the attitude of the civil servants of the Industrial Development Unit of the Department of Trade and Industry, who suggested to Industry Minister Tony Benn and the Cabinet that lending public money to the project was unwise. They felt the paper could not survive and they said so. They adopted the unfavourable report from Chesters and when, despite their recommendation, the loan was agreed, they insisted that their conclusions be included in the prospectus of the newspaper company which, and again at their insistence, was compelled to go public to qualify for loan.

The setbacks, seen as betrayals to the small army in Albion Street united by their common conviction that the enterprise could succeed, could never quite douse their enthusiasm or halt their inch-by-inch uphill progress. If there had been a motto for that thirteen-month struggle, Shelley would have provided it: 'To hope, till hope creates from its own wreck, the thing it contemplates.'

5
The Launch

It had been the shortest run-up to the launch of a daily news-paper in print history. Five weeks from Good Friday, March 28, to the first edition of the first worker-controlled news-paper in Great Britain, May 5. The infant co-operative had taken the building over from Beaverbrook less than three weeks before the first paper was due to roll off the giant Goss presses, which hadn't turned in nearly fourteen months. There were daunting problems to be overcome — ordering of newsprint, the co-ordination of the various production skills which hadn't fused in over a year, the breaking-in of new staff. And in particular the Action Committee, now called the Executive or Works Council, had to settle into the role of running a daily newspaper in the hard commercial world.

In these five weeks from Good Friday to launch, the Works Council had won their first boardroom battle, sanctioned by the whole workforce, to remove Robert Maxwell's executive authority. They had attempted to sever completely his relationship with the *Daily News* but this had been modified at a mass meeting on Thursday, April 17, to stripping him of his executive powers. The workforce now knew that Maxwell had not, in fact, contributed an extra £25,000 on March 28, that £11,000 had come from journalists Ray Chard and Allan Saxton.

The workers deeply resented that Maxwell had imposed last-minute conditions, consolidating his power and imposing his identity on the project. But there was still a residual admiration for the man, for his success and ruth-lessness, but principally because he had put in his capital at a time when others walked away. And although the hardliners on the Works Council, like Charlie Armstrong and Jimmy McNamara, a left-wing engineer, urged the total extinction of Maxwell, whom they accused of trying to get himself a newspaper on the cheap, the mass meeting balked at the *coup de grace*.

The Works Council could reassure themselves, however, in the knowledge that although Maxwell's contribution was the second-largest outside capital investment after Beaverbrook's, his £114,000 gave him no voting power, less say in the running of the company than the cleaner or doorman, whose £100 of employee shares entitled them to ballot their views on the running of the enterprise.

This view, as later events proved, was ingenuous. Control of the company would finally rest with those who could make the most attractive promises to the worker-shareholders on the security of their investment and the continuity of their employment. But on Sunday, May 4, as the great launch moment drew near, there was a mood of conciliation as well as euphoria in Albion Street. Maxwell, still technically co-chairman of the co-operative but without executive power, joined the workers, the celebrities, the politicos from all points of the compass, in celebrating the birth of the *Scottish Daily News*.

The day had started with a large contingent of the staff joining the annual May Day march from Glasgow's George Square to Queen's Park. They had been well received, marching along behind a huge *Scottish Daily News* banner, and along the route in places spectators spontaneously broke into applause. The marchers took the opportunity to hand out hundreds of leaflets, lapel badges and car stickers which pushed the message 'GOOD NEWS IS HERE'. They were tracked by a film crew from the Granada television programme 'World in Action', shooting the final feet of a half-hour documentary which would go out the next night, Monday, Day One of the *Daily News*.

By three o'clock Albion Street was beginning to tick over. Reporters were filing stories, sub-editors were drifting in to begin their shifts and the agency wire services — the life blood of a national newspaper — were beginning to spew out the miles of nightly news from all over the world. Arranging the news wires from the Press Association, Reuters and UPI had not been without its problems — there had been the renegotiating of the contract fixed up by Maxwell with the PA and an inordinate delay while the Post Office connected up the terminals — and it was not until three days before the launch that the system finally became fully operational.

On the night, though, it had all come out right. Copy was coming in, although at a substantially higher cost to the company than Maxwell had arranged. The Press Association supply their news service to subscribers on a sliding scale, governed by circulation. The price Maxwell had obtained was, at £19,000 a year, based on a circulation level of 90,000 and the projected figure for the *Daily News* was 250,000. The Works Council, mindful from the outset that they had to be free of any taint of sharp business practice, worked out a new contract with the PA costing the company £35,000 a year, subject to *pro rata* increases or returns according to actual circulation.

A newsprint contract had also been renegotiated — to the financial detriment of the company Robert Maxwell argued. Charlie Armstrong, the councillor responsible for co-ordinating production, disagrees:

'We were very cautious about the newsprint contract he negotiated because newsprint contracts run into millions of pounds and we had to be in on this.

'Because, look, he's invested a hundred thousand pounds and he goes to someone and negotiates a million-and-a-half newsprint contract and it's easy, as Mr Ten Per Cent, to get his hundred thousand pounds back.

'What happened was that Richard Briston got a letter from a guy called Charles de Selincourt who is the head boy for British International Papers in this country asking to see Professor Briston because he had signed some sort of contract with Robert Maxwell for newsprint. So de Selincourt was in Glasgow and Mackie, Briston and myself had a meeting with him and he had this contract for 12,000 tons of newsprint which was over-ordered for us.

'We'd based everything on a sixteen-page, 200 to 250,000 circulation newspaper and we'd worked it out that we needed about 10,000 tons per annum. Everything was worked out on a sixteen-page broadsheet. There's not a newspaper in the country which buys all its newsprint from one supplier for a start and Maxwell came up with this contract and he'd over-ordered. And all from the same supplier. And that's a very foolish thing to do because you're putting all your eggs in one basket.

'So de Selincourt realised this himself and this is why he asked for the meeting. So we drew up another contract and Mackie signed it that day, that they would supply all our newsprint for the first two months and after that we could go on to another supplier. So then we came back and phoned a company, Press Papers, who we had a meeting with some six months previously. I spoke to this guy at the other end and he said, "We've had a meeting with your Mr Maxwell and we're not prepared to do business." This was the day after Maxwell had lost his executive power, April 18, so I said I would like to apologise on behalf of the people here for any embarrassment that Robert Maxwell caused your company but if you've looked at your newspapers this morning you'll see that the position has changed and that Robert Maxwell no longer has any executive powers.

'So anyway we managed to smooth things over and a few days later we had a meeting with a Mr Ingerville of Press Papers to put him exactly in the position as to what had happened. And we agreed a contract that after two months Press Papers would provide one third of the newsprint and British International two thirds. The benefit of the Press Papers deal was that they have a storage depot at Grangemouth and the paper comes in through Eyemouth or somewhere like that. There was a fishing blockade in 1974 and if that had happened we'd have had no newsprint if we had contracted to them solely.

'Maxwell had implied that he got the paper far, far cheaper but these guys told us that he had got exactly the same deal as anyone else. And as a matter of fact we even got a £2 a ton delivery charge knocked off.'

Maxwell's autocratic management decisions angered more than the Works Council. Eric Tough, a management expert, seconded to the co-operative from PA Management Consultants on his salary of £12,000 a year, clashed head on with him. The wealthy publisher's insistence on several rewrites of the prospectus, supposedly to make it more attractive to potential investors, was the first point of conflict: Tough considered the amendments unnecessary. Then only hours before the end of the three-week push for investment, Maxwell rang up Albion Street to summon Tough and editor Fred Sillitto immediately to London.

'We met Maxwell in his London flat and he said to us: "I'm very worried about this issue. No-one has ever issued a prospectus without its being underwritten and I'm going to be caught in a failure." He was saying that he didn't think that he could put in his £100,000. Then there was a long pause and he said, "Well, if I do put the money in I must have a guarantee that you become my alter egos."

Both men were *ex officio* members of the Executive Council with voting powers. According to Tough, Maxwell was proposing not to honour his commitment of 50p for every worker's pound unless the two men would guarantee to support him 'if it comes to the crunch'.

Tough and Sillitto told Maxwell that they were not prepared to agree to that and returned to Glasgow. Robert Maxwell arrived in Glasgow next day, March 28, apparently having decided to go ahead with his investment — but with conditions.

The incident which really angered Tough came a day or two after the co-operative took over Albion Street from Beaverbrook. Tough had phoned Beaverbrook in Manchester to ask if they could send on fifteen tons of scrap paper to test-run the machines which had been unused for a year. A few minutes later he was phoned back to be told that Maxwell had already ordered all the stocks of scrap paper, 170 tons, and it was on its way to Glasgow.

An hour later Tough was called down to the loading bay to sort out the chaos that had been visited on Albion Street and the surrounding area by the arrival of the paper: 'Every street in the area around the building was blocked with large artic. lorries stacked with paper. And when we looked at the reels we found that one side had already been pre-printed with colour cartoons. It was totally useless so I sent it back.'

The orders placed with the two paper companies at least ensured that there would be paper enough for the launch, but there was a grave shortage of headline typefaces in the caseroom. Most of the families of type had been taken to Manchester after the closure and what was left was either too closely associated with the *Daily Express* typography — the Century face, for instance — or was stylistically outmoded, like Caslon or Ludlow. The Executive Council approached the *Glasgow Herald/Evening Times* management, the only other major letterpress printers in the city, to lend them type until new stocks could be bought; but it never arrived. Rather than order new faces and have capital, to the extent of £3,000 for each family of type, tied up through the six months delivery time, the Works Council decided to make do and amend; one headline face was moulded in metal from negatives created from Letraset stick-down lettering. This manoeuvre was not only ingenious but also a blatant infringement of copyright and a clear breach of union demarcation lines. It was vetoed by the unions. So the make-up of the newspaper had to be a compromise based on the limited typefaces available, and the few dummy newspapers printed before the launch stranded the paper's visual identity somewhere between the *Sunday Express* and the defunct *Evening Citizen*.

Another factor militated against a new and radically different *Scottish Daily News,* the rutted thinking of the paper's editorial management who had no clear conception of what the paper should look like, think or say. Any "fresh air of freedom' blowing through the pages of the *Scottish Daily News,* it quickly became obvious, would not be generated from the editorial summit of Albion Street.

The editorial production of the dummy newspapers had been hampered by the lack of live copy; reporters were concentrating on long-term stories for use in the real newspaper and sub-editors had no wire services to work from. Subs were turning up each morning — in itself an unreal time for these animals to be up and about — to edit stories culled from the 'heavies', transforming dense prose and long sentences into the staccato cliches of the popular newspaper.

In all there were six full dummy newspapers, all of them

produced in the week before the launch, and each night a few hundred copies were run through the huge presses, almost in the blink of an eye. There was tight security throughout the building when these copies came off the presses, they were counted and then distributed department by department and, after scrutiny, locked away again. Despite these measures, copies did find their way out of the building and they turned up in rival newspaper offices.

In the week before the launch all 500 employees were on full pay — for most of them the first wages they had earned in fourteen months. There was an air of unreality about the operations, half-heartedly producing dummies without the pressures and excitement of keeping pace with events in the world outside. There was also growing concern among some of the journalists at the absence of any directions or stimulation from the editor, Fred Sillitto. Requests for editorial meetings to thrash out a style, to define the policies and ethics of the paper beyond the vague phrases in the prospectus, brought no response. Like Topsy, it seemed, the paper was just going to grow haphazardly until it broke out of Albion Street on the night. It was becoming evident that what was going to appear would differ little from what was already available in other newspapers and, indeed, from what had come out of Albion Street under the old management. The indications were, already, that the *Scottish Daily News* would be a tired mix of court reports, deaths and bland features, surrounded by football and national, agency news. Formula journalism, but of another age. The sedate and outmoded blend would, as a market research survey later showed, find its place among the old and elderly, totally failing to penetrate the younger market where newspapers and advertisers focused.

The slack hand on the editorial tiller brought consolation to one section of the editorial, those midnight mafiosi who remained, augmented by a few radical sub-editor recruits, who were concerned that there might be a reversion to type amongst some of their colleagues and an attempt to change the proclaimed left-of-centre direction of the paper. This radical rump was buoyed because there had been no coup from the right, as they saw it, and the *SDN* was still on its committed, if languid, course. This group had a vision of what the paper should be but their

68

power was only to take out what should not be. They could react to the news they received by rewriting it to make it more punchy, dismissive or approving. They could supply vivid headlines, they could strike out cant and jingoism, contract or expand what they were given. But they were always recipients, with the power only of veto or amendment. They had no say on what news stories should be used, what stories should be covered, who should report them or the manner in which that was done. They could not even be sure that the salient points had been included and there was a general contempt for the abilities of most of the reporters. This negative urge was useful to the paper but it needed a more creative force in the shaping of its identity and it quickly emerged that that dynamic was missing.

By eight o'clock on the Sunday evening of the launch, May 4, the tempo which had been quickening throughout the day reached frenzy. The production cycle of a newspaper reaches a jagged pinnacle in the hour before copy deadline for the first edition and that time has the visual appearance of a silent movie with a soundtrack added by Stockhausen. Typewriters hammer, phones jangle, nerves shred, voices are never below one hundred decibel level, radios tuned into police and fire brigade frequencies cackle metallically, copy boys weave between crashing lunacy picking up and dispatching copy. On launch night there were several added constituents, the neon presence of several television crews and the periodic appearance of voyeur-celebrities slowly and obstructively coasting through the melee. The players, sweating under arc lights, smoking incessantly, downing cups of coffee, giving off malevolent vapours, coped with it all — even the dribble of sparkling ladies who minced through, glasses of drink in hand, *en route* to watch the button being pushed to start the run.

Tony Benn, the Industry Minister, was there, as was Robert Maxwell, the latter doing the introductions and the guided tour like a proud father — Allister Mackie seeming to be pulled along in the slipstream. Jimmy Reid, the left-wing UCS shop steward, flanked Teddy Taylor the right-wing Tory MP for Cathcart. William Wolfe, the chairman of the Scottish National Party, nudged Matt McGinn the Glasgow folk-singer and bard to the *Daily News*.

The splash story in the first edition concerned a pretty young girl who had 'died' in a car crash and after being brought back to life had gone on to become a moderately successful model. The headline 'IT'S GREAT TO BE ALIVE' exemplified the mood of the 500 workers who provided their own 'we proved them wrong' piece which ran alongside. It was a poor splash story, particularly for a newspaper which promised to be 'bright but never trivial', more suited to the couthie *Sunday Post* market than a thrusting, finger-on-the-pulse entrant into the daily paper market. The heroine of the piece, Billie Muego, was kept cloistered on the third floor throughout the entire evening lest she be scooped up and carried off into the pages of the *Daily Express* or *Daily Record*.

After all the subbed copy had been sent down the suction tube to the caseroom below where it was set into type, journalists began drifting down to the machine room where a tight crowd was gathering to watch the first paper come off the co-operatively owned presses. The crowd swelled as the projected deadline, 9.50 p.m., approached. Production workers, their part in the operation finished, joined the jostle as the last stereo plate trundled along rollers set in the metal floor of the press bed, crowding in on the nucleus of Robert Maxwell, Allister Mackie and Teresa Docherty, the paper's first public investor, who would push the button to set the rotary presses running. Television crews, from 'World in Action' and the BBC, turned their radium-blue focus on the hub. As the klaxon sounded the all clear, Allister Mackie popped open a bottle of champagne, glasses were filled and handed up to men hanging from the catwalks above. One or two voices shouted 'Let's beat the *Record* on to the streets', two men embraced emotionally while others shook hands, Robert Maxwell roughly pulled Teresa Docherty's face into the full fluorescence of the TV lights before she pressed the button feeding the reeled paper through the inked rotary plates until it came out at the other end, chopped and folded into sixteen broadsheet pages, as the *Scottish Daily News*.

It was good to be alive!

Predictably, the first issue was a sellout. Spirits were high in Albion Street on Monday with 260,000 copies away.

It had been expected that the first few issues would be sold out, more for their souvenir value than anything else. How fast and how far this initial circulation would decline after the first few days was the acid test. There were, however, a number of factors going for the paper — the struggle to launch it had been widely covered by the news media through the thirteen months and, in addition, there had been an advertising barrage on television and commercial radio for several days prior to the launch; the *Scottish Daily Express,* deprived of any free publicity, doubled the *Daily News* advertising budget of £50,000 in its fight to hold on to the readers the *SDN* was struggling for.

The *Daily News* Executive Council had estimated that, after an initially high 'interest circulation' sales would fall back to 220,000 until about three weeks after the launch when, the curiosity element shed and committed readers won, the newspaper would bed into the market. Finally, after two or three months, the target of 250,000 consistent sales would be obtained.

The Strathclyde report had shown that the Scottish public overwhelmingly preferred tabloid newspapers rather than the broadsheet the *Daily News,* through mechanical limitations, was giving them. By and large, most morning papers are bought by people on their way to work and the practical difficulties of coping with the larger paper on public transport are well known. Another factor in the success of tabloid newspapers is the bright way they can present the news: broadsheet make-up tends to be greyer, more bitty, due to the proliferation of stories and typefaces on the page. But despite the desire to produce a tabloid newspaper the workers were stuck with the unpopular-sized broadsheet. Enquiries had been made about whether the presses could be altered to produce a tabloid but the evidence — based on the London *Evening News,* who had converted similar machines — was that it would take eighteen months and cost £160,000. So the thought had been discarded and what proved to be a crucial error by the workers resulted in quantifiable damage to the circulation and the financial stability of the *SDN*. Because the presses could be, and were later, successfully converted in a few hours and at no cost to the co-operative.

But on Monday evening, as the 500 wound into the

71

second day of their joint publishing venture, it seemed that the tabloid versus broadsheet issue was a marginal one. By all the signs the *Daily News* was on its way to success, with a first edition sold out and a stream of visitors and telephone callers congratulating the co-operators on the paper.

At 8.30 that evening, in the middle of the production schedule, the 'World in Action' film was due to go out. In their week at the *Daily News* the Granada crew had been given access to Works Council meetings and editorial meetings, such as they were. The director of the film, Steve Morrison, came from the Glasgow area and although there had been fears that the programme would be constructed to damage the co-operative, Morrison's reassurances had calmed them. By transmission time a large crowd filled Tom's Bar, adjoining the *Daily News,* in the fetid heat to watch the programme.

After a short introduction the film focused on the man who had provided the *Daily News* with its chance, Tony Benn. To cheering and whistling in the bar Benn explained his philosophy:

'Perhaps I'm a watering can in this garden but the flowers are coming up everywhere. I was in Jarrow over the weekend and there the shipyard workers are working on the plan for industrial democracy at Swan Hunter which is going to be brought into public ownership. The Leyland workers in the Midlands are working. My aircraft workers in Bristol have published the most brilliant scheme for industrial democracy in the aircraft industry. In Meriden the motorbikes are being built again. In Kirkby in Liverpool they've got their night storage heaters and their fruit juice and they're planning it. The thing is going like wildfire throughout the country and it's the most exciting thing that's happened in Britain since the war. But the advantage the *Scottish Daily News* has is that it can write about it from its own experience.'

The main section of the film centred on a Works Council meeting in which the editor, Fred Sillitto, seemed to come under attack from the other members present over editorial content: in particular whether the paper should include contributions from the right, from Cathcart Tory MP Teddy Taylor and former Glasgow Sheriff, Harry Pirie.

Jimmy McNamara, a Communist, told Sillitto, 'There's enough papers for Tories in the country. Tories get every other paper. How can an article by Teddy Taylor be left of centre? He's right of right!'

'That page as it stands, Fred,' Allister Mackie added, 'is right wing. With the exception of the leader column which says its left wing. That's what makes it a mockery.'

'We've got guidelines left of centre and if you work within that, my God, it's a tremendous licence you've got,' McNamara said. 'But you must work within left of centre.'

Sillitto's low-key replies did nothing to correct the impression that he was, as editor, being browbeaten into accepting a line handed down to him by the council: 'I think you're forgetting that for the dummy paper we had to put in the paper what we had, even if it happened to be stories like this.'

In the end-piece, Tony Benn concluded on the theme which had dominated the film. He was asked whether he thought journalists were frightened of workers' control because it would control the editor as much as the old proprietors had done.

'No. I think there's all the difference between having the policy of the paper determined by the people who work on it and having it determined by the people who own it. And for journalists and for printers and for all newspaper workers industrial democracy is the chance they've been waiting for.

'I think what happens in the *Daily News* this May will spread quite rapidly throughout Fleet Street and this year and in the years to come.'

The reaction to the programme by the workforce was a general inarticulate anger. They felt that the film was un-representational, deliberately angled to play up drama and conflict. They had trustingly offered their hand to 'World in Action' and had taken it on the chin in return. It is an unwritten rule of the media that criticism is made only of those outside the circle — dog does not eat dog, unless it happens to be particularly feeble — and this canon had been breached: paranoia returned to the inhabitants of the black, glass building in Albion Street. 'World in Action' was to be seen as the sole culprit for the decline in circulation which set in after the first week. And Denny Macgee, one of the assistant editors, would continually return to the programme, his one lucid reason for failure, even at the last mass meeting before the final collapse: the shock waves of that half-hour programme could still be heard reverberating round the building six months later.

But in the first week of publication sales rose steadily to peak at 330,000. Advertising, however, was not coming in at anything like the necessary level, just under 50% of content The executive blamed this on antipathy from advertisers and their agents, based on the paper's proclaimed left-of-centre stance. Although the political complexion of the paper may well have been influential with some advertisers, the truth was probably more prosaic. The *Daily News* advertising department was understaffed and inexperienced, advertising rate cards did not reach the principal agents until three days after the launch and there was a general feeling that the cost of advertising in the paper — £700 a page — was just too high. There was also marked scepticism about the circulation the newspaper was claiming, which was unaudited by any independent body. Lastly, the paper's launch coincided with a devastating recession in advertising which deepened the normal trough in May, after six-month budgets and schedules had been made out. It would be September before the next schedules would be compiled, the lean summer advertising period over.

The second week of publication was haunted by plummeting circulation. By Thursday, when the Federated Chapel (the caucus of the trade union leaders in the building) met for the first time since the launch, the drop in circulation was top of the agenda. The workforce as a whole were not fully aware that the bottom was beginning to drop out. Sales had been kept a close secret between the Works Council and production executives but rumours emanating from the machine room indicated that the hiatus antici- pated in the prospectus had occurred sooner and more disastrously than expected. The Federated Chapel was told that the print run for that morning had been down to 210,000, indicating real sales of less than 200,000.

The Federated Chapel discussed circulation problems: there were only fifteen sales representatives to cover 6,000 retail outlets, news billboards to attract the casual buyer had not arrived, the paper was on a sale or return basis for four weeks at the insistence of the distributors, which meant that

74

Albion Street, Glasgow

Robert Maxwell's cheque, 28 March 1975

Charlie Armstrong on telephone to Tony Benn, who is considering Government loan,
28 March 1975

Allister Mackie

Jimmy McNamara

Denny Macgee

Fred Sillitto

Launch night – Tony Benn, Robert Maxwell, Allister Mackie

Professor Richard Briston

Eric Tough

Fred Sillitto and Nathan Goldberg

Robert Maxwell

Discussing Maxwell's telex – Works Councillors Eric Tough, Allister Mackie, Charlie Armstrong, James Russell

Dorothy-Grace Elder

Alister Blyth and Nathan Goldberg

Robert Maxwell at tannoy

shops were pushing rival papers (like the *Express* and *Record*) which they got nothing back on if they failed to sell. And there was also a suggestion that one of the sub-contractors employed by Menzies, the distributors, had been bought by one of the competitors and was ensuring that his vendors discriminated against the *SDN*.

Alister Blyth, one of two works councillors present, said that these reasons were coupled to a more fundamental factor — the public were simply dissatisfied with the editorial content. His view was supported by electrician Bob McKay who cited disappointed trade union reaction. George Welsh, the journalists' FoC, reacted uncomfortably. The editorial was understaffed, he said, and there were a number of inexperienced members. But that apart, the journalists were having a superhuman task in filling the columns due to the lack of advertising.

Jimmy McNamara, the other works councillor present, also came under fire for his appearance on the 'World in Action' programme. Through it he was accused of doing the co-operative irreparable damage. The Works Council — particularly McNamara and Armstrong — had been seen as confirming right-wing predictions that there would be no editorial freedom under workers' control. George Welsh said' that 'dirty linen had been washed in public', and he rebuked the Works' Council for allowing the film crew to 'run amok' in the building.

The festering resentment in Albion Street — the paranoic siege mentality enforced by the threat of the dole queue — proved fertile to Robert Maxwell when he launched his first bid to recapture his lost authority five days later.

At midnight on Tuesday, May 20, a telex from Pergapress, Oxford, began its eight-foot progress through a teleprinter in the *Daily News* wire room. It was addressed to Allister Mackie and the Works Council, with copies to all the FoCs. It ended 'yours fraternally, Robert Maxwell.' The substance of it was hardly convivial, prophesying the imminent collapse of the newspaper and the loss of 500 jobs if he, Maxwell, was not recalled. A brushfire of alarm immediately raced through the building. The telex read:

I came to help launch the *SDN* workers' co-operative because you and your colleagues and Mr Anthony

Wedgwood Benn asked me to. Over a long period I gave you a considerable amount of my time free and unstintingly and many of my suggestions which the Action Committee followed were certainly instrumental as you yourself have admitted in getting the project off the ground. I was, therefore, surprised to say the least by your attempting to remove me from the co-chairmanship so soon after I had been instrumental in helping you raise the necessary money to get the project launched.

However, I decided that this was your show and that you should be allowed to run things the way you liked. Several times I pointed out that without me or somebody like me you would find it difficult to launch the paper successfully, to maintain its high circulation and get quickly the necessary advertising. You insisted that you could do all this by yourself and 'in any case you should be allowed to make your own mistakes.' As unanimously desired by our workforce I agreed to keep my peace and not rock the boat and I have adhered to this decision.

However, in view of the unexpected gravity of the *SDN's* economic situation, with our sold circulation having fallen as quickly from 325,000 to around 200,000 (which is 50,000 below our prospectus forecast) and our advertising revenue being only 25% instead of the projected 47% of the content of each paper, it would be improper for me to remain silent and sit on the sidelines whilst our workers' co-operative is literally heading for the rocks, with all the loss of jobs that would mean for our staff, the loss of investments to them and all shareholders, not to mention the embarrassment that this would cause the Government and Mr Wedgwood Benn in particular, were this ghastly situation allowed to happen.

Maxwell then went into a detailed summary of what he called 'our present precarious position':

After purchasing the building and plant, our co-operative started off with an ample bank balance of £950,000 which I estimated would be sufficient to see us through for an eighteen-month period from date of launch. Thus giving us sufficient time to secure our viability in the market. Since the launch we have spent approximately £250,000 on publicity, spares, lawyers, accountants, motor cars, telephones, wages and sundry expenses etc. Leaving us with some £700,000. Just before the launch you, contrary to my specific advice, made the disastrous deal for newsprint which involved us in depositing in a blocked account £200,000 as security for payment of bills instead of getting the newsprint on credit as I had negotiated. This left us with just over £500,000 in hand.

Our current costs per six-day week are £90,000 without making any provision for interest on borrowed money or for dividends. The weekly expenditure of £90,000 is made up as follows:

Wages and salaries	£30,000
Newsprint	£36,000
Other overheads including depreciation	£24,000

Our income, assuming that we can hold our circulation at net sales of 200,000 over the difficult summer months is as follows:

Sales of the *SDN*	£45,000
Net advertising revenue per week	£12,000
Making weekly total of	£57,000

Again, it must be pointed out that the advertisements and circulation managers and all of us will have to work extremely hard and be very lucky to hold the present circulation and achieve the advertising revenue of £12,000 per week over this very difficult period. £30,000 is our present weekly loss.

Our total income from *SDN* sales and ads being £57,000 and our total weekly expenditure being £90,000, this means that we are at present running the company at a loss in excess of £30,000 per week.

With our free cash in hand being only some £500,000 you must readily see that unless immediate drastic action is taken to re-launch the paper both to quickly bring up its sales to 250,000 plus copies (thus increasing our weekly income from that source from its present £12,000 to £21,000) our present cash resources

77

will be exhausted between 15th September and 31st October of this year. I am sure that you, the council, the workforce and all shareholders (including the Department of Industry) will agree that this cannot be allowed to happen.

I have verified the above financial figures with our general manager Mr Eric Tough. He agrees that they are approximately right on the present circulation of 200,000 and our advertising revenue being £12,000 per week. However, he believes that we will succeed in getting our advertising revenue to £21,000 per week. He has not been able to tell me as to how he and the council propose to achieve this although I am sure he will do his best to help.

We must all view this situation with the utmost gravity and I call upon you and the council to call this week a meeting of our full workforce so as to take them into our confidence and to ask for their advice and assistance, whilst at the same time outlining the council's plan on how we propose to save the *SDN* and the first workers' co-operative in the newspaper industry from probable total collapse well before the end of this year.

I know that your immediate reaction will be to accuse me of panic-mongering. This accusation would be as untrue as it is undeserved. The figures I quote are facts as verified with the general manager and anybody with a pencil and a piece of paper can quickly work out that on our present circulation and advertising figures (which unless we take some immediate special steps to improve them are likely to fall) this company will, within less than six months, be unable to meet its wages and other commitments.

I have some concrete proposals which may just save the situation, the key being to make it possible for the editor and his staff to produce a much better and exciting newspaper. This can only be done by increasing the journalistic staff and, where appropriate, also in the caseroom to bring about better editioning. I also have suggestions as to how we can try to reverse immediately this disastrous fall in advertising.

Finally, I have concrete proposals, that will cost very

little money, to increase immediately our circulation representation staff throughout Scotland which is so necessary if we are to get our circulation up quickly above 250,000 and so critical to our survival. In order to implement these, the Executive Council will have to give me the necessary approval and authority to carry out jointly with you, our management and staff these urgent measures.

It is very easy to see why your unnecessary 'World in Action' television appearance showing the works' council's gross interference in editorial affairs, coupled with the originally set uncompetitive advertising rates and your overturning my approved suggestion that we should launch the paper at 5p so that the Scottish people would have (until autumn) a monetary incentive to buy us rather than the *Scottish Daily Express*, has unwittingly endangered the future existence of the *SDN*. The lack of paid advertising (you prohibited me from helping to organise a meeting with the main London advertising agencies and advertisers which has meant that I am unable to assist our hard-working advertisement manager in achieving success in this field), is necessarily putting great pressure on our slender NUJ and caseroom staff. They are just not in a position to fill virtually all the pages with copy and even if by some superhuman effort they succeed this results in many pages being a grey and unattractive mass.

In view of the grave danger which our enterprise finds itself in, I hope you will cease your stubborn refusal to comply with the letter and spirit of the workforce meeting's decision and agree to let us all work together to save the paper and its 500 jobs. We have barely four weeks to save the situation because after the end of June we enter the traditional period when newspapers lose circulation and when advertising is even harder to obtain than at present.

In conlusion since you have refused so far to convene a mass meeting of our workforce and since I have no assurance that you will convene it now I have copied this telex to the FoCs so that they may inform their respective chapels of our present very serious position.

The Works Council met next morning to discuss the long and accusatory telex. Allister Mackie, in short-sleeved sports shirt, took the chair. Next to him was Eric Tough the general manager. Mackie opened:

'Okay lads, you know the most important item on the agenda. It's this telex we've received from Bob Maxwell and in it he's saying some rather alarming things.'

The men set about dispelling the ugly clouds Maxwell had conjured up, while brilliant early summer sunlight streamed through the window of the boardroom. On the first point, Maxwell's claim that the circulation was off-target with the prospectus was rebutted.

"We didn't expect to get up to 250,000 till after three months," Jim Russell said.

'If anything we're slightly higher than schedule,' Tough added.

They moved on to the state of the company's finances, agreeing with Maxwell that there was a cash balance of £950,000 after the purchase of Albion Street, brought down to £717,000 by spares, legal and launching expenses.

'And then Bob makes a comment that it was a disastrous deal for the newsprint which involved us depositing £200,000 in security,' Mackie read.

Not so, Tough replied. Newsprint was the biggest single expense and the biggest problem. Supplies were now guaranteed with the setting aside of the money. And the cost of the newsprint, at £10 a ton, was less than was forecast in the prospectus.

That left £500,000, invested with the City of Glasgow. The claim that the current costs of running the company were £90,000 was also disputed. In his calculation Maxwell had used the fixed cost of producing a sixteen-page broadsheet with a print of 300,000. Whereas the *SDN* was printing only 200,000, often of a fourteen-page paper. The newsprint cost was therefore not £36,000 but £21,000, Tough told the council. Maxwell had also exaggerated wages and fixed costs by a total of £8,000 a week.

Income to the co-operative, Mackie calculated, would be £45,000 from sales if the *Daily News* could hold circulation through the lean summer months and advertising income, based on the amounts sold in the first two weeks of the paper, would run at £20,000 a week.

In all, Tough told the Works Council, Maxwell had exaggerated expenses by over £20,000 and underestimated income by £10,000. 'We are, as we forecast, just about breaking even. He's overstated costs and understated revenue. And there's your £30,000. That is the explanation of the situation.'

The Works Council was satisfied that the figures were wrong. They listened to Tough telling them that Maxwell was also incorrect in saying that he had verified them. It was, Tough said charitably, a misunderstanding based on a quick telephone conversation. What Maxwell had done was to pick out some figures which applied to a 300,000 circulation, some which applied to a 200,000 circulation, others which included newsprint, others which didn't. 'And he has got it wrong, as you're bound to if you do it that way.'

There only remained the problem of remedying the damage in confidence that the dissemination of the telex had caused. 'He has affected the morale of the workforce,' Mackie said testily, 'by telling them that they're going to be out of a job by October 31.'

At four that afternoon the Works Council, with Eric Tough, met the Federated Chapel to set about repairing morale. They reminded the FoCs that Tony Benn had not asked Robert Maxwell to help in the launch of the *SDN* and indeed, according to the councillors, had actually warned them off Maxwell. The Federated Chapel minuted their displeasure of Maxwell's allegation that he had been dropped because the employees wanted to run the show — 'as all employees remember, we dropped him because he decided it was not our show'. Maxwell was further condemned for undermining the confidence of the workforce. And it was moved that 'he should not be allowed to interfere with the running of the company.'

Despite the factual errors in the telex, despite the probability of the company, at that point, still being in the black, the underlying trend had still not been recognised. In the first two days of the third week the print figures had dropped another 20,000, to 190,000, which meant that the actual sales figure, after returns were taken into account, was below 180,000 and dropping. And for the first time a wedge had been driven between the executive of the paper and the workforce. The Fathers of the Chapels would go back to their membership satisfied that the Maxwell figures were inaccurate, and the workforce would agree at a mass meeting later that week that the figures Eric Tough put to them were correct. But they could read the signs and once more the dole-fear was crystallising in Albion Street.

6
The Co-operative

In a discussion document issued to the members of the *Scottish Daily News* workforce by the Action Committee before the launch of the newspaper the committee outlined their view of what a workers' co-operative would mean, in practice:

'In our workers' co-operative it must be emphasised to the workforce that this is *their* factory, producing *their* newspaper. It is anticipated that once this truth is wholly absorbed, the workforce will themselves come to realise that confrontation, as we have all previously understood it, becomes an anachronism, a thing of the past.

How can one confront oneself? The position is as basic and as simple as this question. No longer is there a *them* and *us* situation. We control and operate *our* newspaper, and we co-ordinate our efforts and our thinking to this end.

Obviously the traditional union demarcation lines for jobs will continue, only we expect that chapels will themselves have a look at practices within their own areas. For example, we would anticipate that, in the caseroom, it would not be inadmissible for a floor-hand to help out in the lino (the Linotype typesetting machines); in the editorial, a news sub-editor could lend a hand to a sports sub; and so on throughout the building, given union consent.

The workers will work together to the common aim — the success of the *Scottish Daily News*.

It is agreed among many of the most active participants in the *Scottish Daily News* that the project operated as a workers' co-operative, in the full sense of that phrase, for only two months, during April and May 1975, the two months on either side of the launch. Those who latterly supported Maxwell's presence at the helm will insist that his role as chief executive, and his method of implementing that role, were not incompatible with the idea of a workers' co-operative: after all the workforce put him there and the workforce could, at any time, remove him. But those who had a clear conception of what a workers' co-operative ought to be were also clear that an overall boss figure, especially one as dominant as Maxwell, could not fit it.

It should be remembered, however, that the people with a clear vision of a workers' co-operative and a political perspective into which that vision could be fitted, were very much in the minority amongst the 500 workers in Albion Street. For most of the workforce — as for several members of the original action committee — the notion of the former Beaverbrook workers running their own newspaper was simply a last resort.

When the *Scottish Daily Express* closed down, all efforts by the workforce were directed at trying to find an alternative proprietor to take over the business and only when it became clear that no other newspaper proprietor had any interest in buying up the Albion Street building as a going concern, was the idea of the workers buying and operating it themselves conceived. The initial motivation — and the only motivation for most of the workforce — was saving jobs; the fact that the jobs were to be in a worker-controlled enterprise was incidental. Most of the participants had no broad political interest in proving that orthodox capitalist ownership and management could be replaced within a capitalist society by what would, in effect, be an island of industrial democracy in a hostile commercial ocean.

Certainly, once the decision to try to launch a co-operatively owned paper had been taken, many members of the workforce took up the broad cause of workers' control with gusto. They had to convince their trade union colleagues, a Labour Government and other potential supporters that their project had a serious political intention and that it would, if successful, point the way towards a new era in British industrial relations. For some, this represented a genuine conversion from political apathy under Beaverbrook to a certain radical idealism; for others it was a wholly cynical expedient to create jobs for themselves.

That is one reason why the *Scottish Daily News* was never a pure experiment in worker control. Even the financial structure of the enterprise made it clear that the participants were ambivalent about why they were setting off on this unprecedented adventure. The 500 workers were, it could be argued, mini-capitalists embarking on a project of mutual financial benefit, not attempting to offer an alternative to the orthodox capitalist method of funding an enterprise. Certainly, the fact that the workers were putting up £200,000 of their own money as capital was crucial to the initial success in starting the *Scottish Daily News;* it meant that the workers had given an earnest of their own determination, and it guaranteed that they would throw themselves into the project with added enthusiasm because they had something concrete, in addition to their jobs, to lose should the project fail.

Leaving aside the matter of Robert Maxwell, therefore, the *Scottish Daily News* was very far from being a straightforward attempt by politically motivated idealists to create a model alternative to capitalist control of the means of production. Alister Blyth, latterly chairman of the Executive Council of the newspaper, made this position clear in the final weeks of the project, when it was obvious that liquidation was imminent and the Government had refused any form of help.

'Our primary concern', he told a news conference, 'is, as it has always been, to save as many jobs as possible. If the workers' co-operative cannot continue, the workforce would not object to the building and plant being taken over by a newspaper proprietor and used to run a newspaper along orthodox commercial lines'.

It was not by any means an unworthy position to take up. Blyth had never claimed to be a political evangelist and there was nothing objectionable about workers trying to save their jobs. But the dichotomy between those who believed in the workers' co-operative as such, and those who saw the co-operative merely as a necessary expedient to preserving 500 jobs, meant that the project had the seeds of conflict in it from the start. The dichotomy showed at all stages of the project and in many ways — in executive council meetings, in editorial meetings, in the inconsistent content of the paper and in the bitter breakdown of relations within the workforce which several times threatened to flare into violence.

But back in April 1974, the body of workers made redundant by Beaverbrook were unanimous in their support of their Action Committee's proposal to launch their own newspaper. The Action Committee consisted of the fathers of the various Albion Street chapels with Imperial Father of the Federated Chapels Allister Mackie as chairman.

The leading political idealists were Allister Mackie, James McNamara and James Russell, all long-serving members of the Action Committee of the original Executive Council. Nathan Goldberg appeared to straddle the gap between the political idealists and the others, claiming a far-left pedigree and membership of the Communist Party while, at the same time, being Maxwell's principal supporter and confidant. This is not to say that none of the other leading figures had political ideals, merely that their primary motivation appeared to be preserving Albion Street as a going concern, whatever the financial structure of the enterprise or journalistic content of the product.

On May 2, 1974, the action group of ex-Beaverbrook workers submitted its views on the management structure of the proposed newspaper to a working party chaired by Lord Provost of Glasgow (now Sir) William Gray. This began:

The management structure of the enterprise will be based on three precepts:

1. Management will be left to managers.
2. An agreed disputes procedure will be laid down to which all chapels will agree; and
3. Overall management (i.e., company policy, direction etc.,) will be by a works council comprising, members of the top management and employees, with the employees having a majority vote.

Although the final structure must be negotiated with the appointed general manager, we see these guidelines operating on a basis:

1. Once a general manager is appointed he will be expected to get on with the job of managing. No restrictions must be placed in his way on his operations,

but it must be understood that he will at all times be answerable to the Works Council.

2. Basic reasons for disputes (i.e. wages, differentials and working conditions) ought to vanish with the setting-up of an employees' enterprise. However, it must be acknowledged that disputes can also arise from petty reasons. Should any grievance be felt by a chapel, that chapel shall take the complaint to a standing disputes committee that shall be appointed by and shall report back to the Federated Chapel. All chapels shall, by agreement, be members of the Federated Chapel.

Failing the resolving of the grievance by the disputes committee the Federated Chapel shall then investigate the grievance and attempt to resolve it. We anticipate that very few grievances could fail to be resolved at this level, however, in such an event the Works Council shall make itself available. Should this further right of redress fail then a meeting of the appropriate branch secretaries shall be convened to give final judgment. The chapel shall then be deemed to have exercised its right of appeal to its limit and shall be bound to accept this finding as final.

3. The Works Council shall consist of five members of top management and seven employees. One of the employees shall be appointed chairman of the council. The Works Council shall determine overall policy of the Company (i.e., replanting etc.).

4. Another council, Representatives Council, shall be formed. This council shall consider day-to-day production problems. It will be formed of FoCs (Fathers of Chapels) and middle management. This council will have the right to make decisions but not contrary to those of the Works Council.

The Action Committee was, understandably, anxious to convince potential investors and other supporters that the *Scottish Daily News* would be free from the persistent industrial disputes which had crippled the *Scottish Daily Express*. Hence they stressed the existence of an agreed disputes procedure. In the event, of course, the disputes procedure was never put to the test; the workforce were always far too busy producing the newspaper, attending meetings or wheeling and dealing to think of pursuing internal disputes through this cumbersome procedure.

This submission by the Action Committee does, however, reveal the shallowness of the thinking about the role of management. The relationship between the Works Council and the proposed Representatives Council is left mercifully obscure, although the problems it posed were not lost to the Strathclyde feasibility team:

> Our view of this type of management is that there could be an excess of committee discussion when action is needed. The day-to-day running of a business such as a newspaper demands rapid decision-making, often in uncertainty. The decision may be a choice of one of several alternatives and once it has been made it is probably implemented so rapidly as to preclude any second thoughts. In such circumstances group decision-making can at the best be time-consuming and at the worst time-wasting and ineffective.

Iain Bain, looking back on his fourteen weeks as Financial Controller, thought there were two main differences between the co-operative and an ordinary business: the workers were kept very much better informed of what was happening, and there were far too many meetings:

> 'There were certainly too many meetings of the Executive Council and there was far too much aimless talk and argument at these meetings. But I put that down to inexperience more than anything else. I think in time these meetings could have been curtailed and they could have been, of themselves, crisper and more to the point.'

And the Industrial Development Unit of the Department of Trade and Industry recognised an even more damaging flaw in the proposed management structure when they said in their damning report: '. . . there must be questions as to the willingness of the proposed Executive Council to allow the essential freedom of action to the General Manager and Editor, particularly when management decisions prove unpopular with sections of the workforce. Clearly no newspaper can operate successfully if day-to-day management decisions are subject to constant debate.' Regrettably, the IDU's prediction was all too accurate. The Action

Committee's exposition of the freedom of management was a miracle of optimism, when it suggested that once a manager was appointed he would be 'expected to get on with the job of managing. No restrictions must be placed in his way on his operations, but it must be understood that he will at all times be answerable to the Works Council.'

The contradiction in this hopeful suggestion is glaring: how can a manager get on with the job if he is at all times answerable to the Works Council? It might have worked in practice, however, if the majority of the Works Council had had a clear idea of where day-to-day management stopped and policy-making began. They do not appear to have worked out this division effectively. General manager Eric Tough found that policy-making extended down to matters like the price of pies in the canteen and neither he nor any of the other managers ever felt they had the freedom 'to get on with the job'.

In the final version of the management structure as outlined in the prospectus for Scottish News Enterprises Limited, the early model had been considerably modified, but leaving intact the basic premise that the main policy-making body would be controlled by representatives of the workers.

The two governing bodies of the company were the Executive Council and the Investors' Council. The Executive Council had complete control over the management of the company (subject only to the specific powers reserved to the Investors' Council) and consisted of up to ten members: the General Manager and Editor *ex officio*; two members appointed by the Investors' Council; and six members elected by the employees.

The original members of the Executive Council were: Allister Mackie (co-chairman), James Russell, Charles Armstrong, James McNamara, James Lindsay and Alister Blyth as employee representatives; Eric Tough and Fred Sillitto *ex officio;* Robert Maxwell (co-chairman) and James Jack, General Secretary of the Scottish Trade Union Congress as representatives of the Investors' Council. The Investors' Council had up to eight members: the General Manager *ex officio,* two members elected by the Executive Council and the remainder elected by the ordinary shareholders in annual meeting.

The Investors' Council only had two functions, the election of two representatives to the Executive Council and to report, as necessary, to the ordinary shareholders. The Investors' Council was also given certain narrow powers of veto in matters relating to the expansion of the capital of the company and the disposal of profits. Needless to say, these veto powers were never exercised and the Investors' Council played no noticeable part in the story of the *Scottish Daily News*.

One other body might have been expected to play a significant role — the Federated Chapel, the umbrella body of the various trade union branches operating in the newspaper. This consists of the fathers of each of the chapels. However, because of the peculiar relationship between workers and management in the *Scottish Daily News*, the Federated Chapel was disarmed and largely ineffective. The main weapon of the orthodox Federated Chapel, the threat or reality of a disruption of production, was inappropriate: the workforce knew that one stoppage of production would be enough to kill the newspaper and, whatever traditional trade union practices might be breached in Albion Street, neither individual chapels nor the federated Chapel could threaten anything.

Certainly at various points the Federated Chapel attempted to flex its muscles, as when it passed a motion at the height of the Mackie-Maxwell conflict, censuring both men for their public utterances and banning any future statements; the prohibition was ignored by both men.

In practice, then, the Executive Council ruled supreme and the point of conflict within the enterprise was not, as usual, between organised labour and management but between the worker-representatives on the Executive Council and the professional managers.

Eric Tough believes that this conflict was inevitable because of the workers' domination of the main policy-making body — the Executive Council. As general manager he was the only professional manager on the council and found his attempts to introduce a 'more realistic commercial attitude' into policy falling on deaf ears. When he suggested that the content of the paper in the first month had a left-wing bias which was having a disastrous effect on advertising prospects he was told, sharply, that the *Scottish Daily News* was more than just a commercial enterprise, and if principle conflicted with commercial expediency principle would take precedence. It was a frustrating position for Tough, finding himself overruled in commercial matters by men who had no experience of the commercial world.

'The domination of workers on the Executive Council is one of the things I would like to have tried to change if we had been able to get round to matters like that. I saw a huge educational programme that had to be done before these guys would get away from the emotive idea of workers' *control*. We might have aspired to that after a year or two, with them learning the nuts and bolts of running a business. But to expect them to make viable commercial decisions straight away was an awful lot to hope for.

'The Action Committee said often — they said it to me, they said it in the prospectus — Oh, no, we won't interfere with management, we'll fix policy and we'll leave management to run the day-to-day business!

'What they never attempted to find out in their own minds was how they separated out policy from day-to-day business. And in fact everything became policy. The price of pies, the design of notepaper, everything.

'For instance, we wanted a competitions manager. I interviewed someone who had experience and seemed a good man for the job. Then, at the next executive meeting I was told, "There's this chap in the caseroom who could do the job, you'll have to interview him." He'd never done it before, he had no record of ever having done anything like this, but he was "a great chap". They said we had to have him, I said I didn't think so, but it went to a vote and that was that.

'They never got past the stage of thinking and acting like an Action Committee: it's what I called the "wooden hut syndrome" (the wooden hut occupied by the Action Committee during the thirteen-month struggle to raise money for the newspaper).

'The trouble was that the Action Committee who had worked so hard over all that time to keep the thing going were one kind of person, and they did that job terribly well. It was just possible they were quite the wrong people then to go on and run the company. Initially the six worker-directors were just six of the Action Committee, elected *by* the Action Committee. That was another emotive decision. The workers said, "Well, they've done so much to keep the thing going we can't heave them out now." But they should have.

'The people who had run the campaign had been living, eating and sleeping in that hut. They could meet whenever they wanted, and they did. But they carried the same thing over into the newspaper world; they still practically lived in the building so they could — and did —meet five times a day, reversing decisions taken earlier in the day, making it impossible for the managers to get on with the job. They'd say to me over and over again, "O.K., we'll look after policy, you look after day-to-day management!" But if you take away ordering newsprint, ordering letterheads, deciding the layout of the ledger books, hiring a competitions manager, fixing salaries, what the hell is day-to-day running? What's left for me to do?

'If only, you see, they had gone for the middle road, for worker-participation with a policy-making body equally representing workers and management, then the two sides could have gone off to implement policy through their respective — and entirely different — skills. What the *Scottish Daily News* failed completely to do was let the professionals get on with implementing their part of agreed policy. As Allister Mackie said: "We distrust anyone in a suit and white collar." '

With the history of bitterly hostile relations between workers and management under Beaverbrook, that is probably not surprising. And the workers had a justifiable pride in ownership and determination to show the world that they could run their paper themselves. And moreover, those who brought political idealism into their view of the *Scottish Daily News* could justifiably argue that according to Tough's narrow commercial criteria it would not matter whether the paper that emerged from Albion Street was ultra-left or ultra-right so long as it found a market and found advertisers. That would hardly have satisfied the grand promises made for the paper before it appeared.

'I remember one guy,' [Tough recalled] 'now I admire that chap in many ways, who got up at a mass meeting, trembling with emotion and said, "Our current management is even more crooked than Beaverbrook ever was," because we had put our circulation figures in the paper the previous night saying "300,000 and still rising," when it was 250,000 and still falling. He demanded that, as an honest workers' operation, we should retract this. I told them that if they wanted to announce the real figure they could forget advertising, for ever. Every newspaper management cooks the circulation figures—you can't survive without doing it. You have to tell lies, white lies, black lies, any kind. Now this was an educational problem and I think, given time, it could have been overcome. But time was the thing we never had.'

It is clear, then, that in the period during April and May 1975 the management structure of the newspaper was throwing up a number of tensions and was not working very efficiently. Everyone now admits that there were far too many meetings, especially of the Works Council and that management was not being allowed to manage in the way that Eric Tough, at least, would have liked.

It would, however, be grossly unfair to leave the impression that the whole project was in chaos because of the inexperience of the worker-directors. The achievement of reconsecrating the Albion Street building and, in a period of four weeks, bringing the plant and workforce up to the point of producing a newspaper can hardly be overestimated. No newspaper has been launched in anything approaching such a short period and the entire workforce, led by the worker-directors, were throwing themselves into the task with great enthusiasm and efficiency.

It is difficult for those who have never been involved in newspaper management or production to appreciate the complexity of setting up a plant ready to print a daily newspaper. Materials — paper, ink, metal, typefaces and a host of small items down to typewriter ribbons — had to be bought; machines which had lain idle for over a year had to be overhauled and tested; distribution had to be arranged; heating, lighting, telephones and wire services had to be negotiated; staff had to be hired, journalists had to start stock-piling stories and features for the launch period and pre-launch publicity had to be arranged. Behind that first edition of the *Scottish Daily News* on May 5 lay a super-human effort by the workforce. And although most of the workers knew what they were doing because of their long experience under Beaverbrook, the organisation and co-ordination of all this effort stands as an impressive testimony to the efficiency of the co-operative management.

'The things achieved by the workers,' [said Professor Briston in retrospect] 'haven't received the right amount of attention. When you consider, for example, that they began the paper after having been in the building for only four weeks and that they changed to tabloid in a matter of a week or ten days, it is clear that something very remarkable was happening. These things couldn't have been achieved in Fleet Street with-out six months' negotiations, new wage structures and all sorts of other things.'

In fact, one of the reasons why the *Scottish Daily News* appeared first in broadsheet form, a disastrous mistake as it turned out, was that the *Evening News* had taken eighteen months to convert the same kind of machines from broad-sheet to tabloid and had paid out £160,000 to effect the conversion. The *Daily News* made the change in a week or two and at no cost at all.

Towards the end of May it was becoming clear to the Works Council that the initial euphoria which had carried the project through the critical launch period would have to be replaced with an efficient management system which would set a pattern for the long term. The council had been persuaded, by Eric Tough, to hand over day-to-day control to the managers and, although it was a wrench for the worker-directors to delegate any responsibility, they agreed to the change.

At this point the original conception, of the Executive Council dealing with policy matters and management dealing with day-to-day implementation of policy, was just beginning to fall into place. Production of the newspaper was continuing with admirable efficiency and there was not so much as a hint of the atrocious labour-management relations that had characterised the Beaverbrook era.

'When the management represent the workforce,' [explained Allister Mackie at the time] 'they cease being faceless boards of directors and then you have complete rapport between management and workers. The workforce themselves are so cost-conscious that they know that management's problems are also their problems.'

But two dark clouds were already visible on the horizon, starting to obscure the euphoric glow in Albion Street. Sales were refusing to level out, forcing the co-operative to face the unpalatable fact that the *Scottish Daily News* was not a good enough newspaper to hold its readers' attention and loyalty. And, at the same time, Robert Maxwell was beginning to stir again from his exile in Oxford, generating spasms of panic amongst the workforce with his prophecies of doom and forcing the Executive Council to neglect pressing problems and turn, instead, to defending their precious co-operative from the threat of a Maxwell takeover.

June 4, 1975 and the re-election of Robert Maxwell to the Executive Council marked the end of the period when the *Scottish Daily News* was a co-operative in the sense originally intended by the Action Committee. The shortcomings in the management system which had been thrown up over the previous two months were never solved and this was why Eric Tough looked back on the whole project bitterly disappointed that a fascinating experiment was never allowed to reach its conclusion.

7

What the Paper Said

Fred Sillitto was a man who left little impression on the paper he edited and few memories among the journalists he worked with. Everyone spoke well of him, he was a decent and humane man: and no one knew him.

He had been a compromise choice as editor, drafted by the two men who would not accept each other in the editor's chair — Nathan Goldberg and Denny Macgee. Goldberg, at 31, was a personable, experienced sub-editor with a flair for make-up and splash headlines; Macgee was the seasoned trade unionist turned manager. The two had in common a driving ambition and a hectoring fluency at meetings which resulted in a verbal stand-off when neither could gain a majority with their colleagues in the Action Committee days.

The third journalist on the Action Committee, financial reporter James Russell, remembers arriving back from a visit to Robert Maxwell in Oxford to be told that an editor had been chosen, Fred Sillitto. 'Fine,' said Russell. 'Who is Fred Sillitto?'

There are few clues to the editorial personality of the man. He had been appointed deputy editor of the *Scottish Sunday Express*, a sober and characterless mish-mash of a paper, just three months before the closure of Albion Street. Those who worked beside him regarded Sillitto as a skilled operator and a fundamentally decent man, an introspective and private person whose skills did not extend to motivating others or to controlling and shaping the identity of a paper. *Daily Express* sub-editors who worked weekly shifts on the Sunday paper were aware of Fred Sillitto on the back bench, wreathed in cigarette smoke, his head down over the copy, pencilling in and deleting at a steady pace, the glare of the fluorescent lights striking his bald head, while all about him was chaos and tension.

Possibly Fred Sillitto did not want to edit the *Scottish Daily News*. He was not first choice: Charles Graham, a *Scottish Daily Express* columnist who had been retained by Beaverbrook after the closure (and who managed to reconcile membership of the Labour Party with writing right-wing opinions), had been approached. And Michael Cudlipp, nephew of Sir Hugh Cudlipp, had been pencilled in for consideration. He had spent six weeks helping the Action Committee in the barren early days. His acuteness, coupled with his poise and command, had impressed the men. But neither of them could, or would, take the job. It fell to Fred Sillitto.

One of Sillitto's first editorial tasks was to express the character of the projected paper in the prospectus which the *Daily News* had to issue as a condition of releasing the Government's loan.

The new paper would be 'first and foremost a NEWSpaper,' [he wrote], 'telling it straight, simply and objectively: bright but not trivial, responsible but never pompous. It will present the latest in local, national and world events with style and vigour — but without seeking to make the humdrum or routine seem sensational. A newspaper with a sense of value and proportion.

It will be a sporting paper that caters for as many interests as possible, including minority activities. It will remain unconvinced that a footballer with a sore toe has first claim upon the nation's sympathy. But it will view the sports scene with enthusiasm and proper respect for the gifted and heroic without forgetting that basically sport is supposed to be fun and not the most important thing in life.

It will be a political paper seeking to mirror as closely as possible the feelings of the people of Scotland — with a philosophy left of centre. It will provide an open forum for discussion on conflicting policies and viewpoints.

Above all it will not bore its readers with turgid polemics but will speak out with candour and gusto in the space reserved for the paper's own comments.

The fresh air of freedom will blow through its pages. It will aim to provide something for all age groups, from school children to pensioners — and no one will have to hide it from the family. But the interests and aspirations of youth on whom the future of our country depends will receive special attention.

The intention is that everyone will find it entertaining and readable — and that they will buy it and go on buying it because they like it . . . and trust it.

He could have added — but did not — that the paper would be all things to all men. But these few paragraphs, in their antique, sub-Madison Avenue Style, were the only parameters laid down by the editor to his staff in the run-up to the launch, or subsequently. Journalists were being forced to work in an editorial vacuum.

In the week before the launch on May 5, 1975, six dummy newspapers were produced. The first came off the presses at around 11 pm on Sunday, April 27. Four hundred copies were run off to be distributed throughout the building, then the machines were stopped.

Typographically the front page was a hotch-potch of confused and conflicting headline types. It was spotted with one-paragraph shorts which had been pushed in to fill holes left by inexperienced sub-editors whose judgment on the length of stories was faulty. Running alongside the distinctive *Scottish Daily News* masthead and the thistle logo was a 'vital message from the Editor.' Fred the Ed, as he had become known, was appealing to the workforce for unity and for absolute secrecy about the dummy:

The purpose of the dummies is to enable all production, advertising and commercial departments to simulate their own roles in preparation for the moment when the paper goes live.

These dummies will have, at first, many flaws and may reveal gaps and snags in our routine which have not been foreseen. But that is the object of the operation. We are in the throes of organising the fastest-ever launch of any national newspaper in history.

All depends on the total co-operation and goodwill of every department, group and individual involved. We cannot allow ourselves to be diverted from our main purpose by any minor or internal side-issues. We are in the process of making history. Let us do it with harmony and with dignity.

The dummy paper's main story (the 'splash') was a report on the beleaguered South Vietnam capital of Saigon. It was datelined '*Daily News* Reporter, SAIGON, Monday,' and topped by the banner headline 'A Heartbeat from Saigon'. In fact the story had been pieced together from radio and television news bulletins and dressed up by Nathan Goldberg who was now deputy editor in charge of editorial production (his rival Denny Macgee occupied a parallel position as deputy editor in charge of administration).

The first paragraph read: 'Terror and confusion grips this city tonight as the Communist ring of steel closes even more tightly. And it became intensified as shooting broke out inside the South Vietnamese capital.' Alongside was a grey picture of a group of people, presumably Vietnamese, backs to the camera and scurrying away.

At the bottom of the page a four-inch double column precis of the night's television caught the eye of the reader-viewer too lazy to turn to Page 10 where TV and radio were covered at inordinate length.

Since the *Daily News* had no prepared policy and a total lack of political and editorial guidance, the selection of news, its prominence and the way it was treated depended on the whim or prejudice of the individual journalist.

Thus, in the dummy, an unchaperoned sub-editor could create a Communist ring of steel which was unable to suppress the beating heart of a people, while on another night the freedom-fighting Vietcong would be liberating the shackled populace. Ironically, the creative freedom which the journalists enjoyed — a unique opportunity to produce a newspaper of their own style and reflecting their own convictions — resulted merely in an inconsistent newspaper, an unhappy rag-bag of opinions and eccentric stories. The editorial hierarchy never managed to harness the conflicting forces under firm guidelines, never created a policy and a treatment of news which was fresh or radical or even consistent. Fred Sillitto, at sixty, knew all about the newspaper industry. In fact knew it all too well. What was needed was an editor with a fresh vision, without conditioned responses, who could reflect and report the rapidly changing social and political nature of Scotland. The new newspaper, which promised to concentrate on young people and to speak out with candour and gusto, was shaping up to be doddering and equivocal.

On Page 2, Allan Saxton, with forty-five years on the *Scottish Daily Express* behind him, was the self-styled Chief Foreign Sub-Editor. This page was dominated by a four-column photograph of the Queen in Jamaica and, below, Ted Whitehead, a wordy and opinionated reporter based in the tiny London office, had put together an article about the political future of Portugal with dire warnings about those who 'are crying wolf and reds under the bed.'

But it was Fred Sillitto's leader page which was the real litmus test.   Alongside his editorial, 'The Start of a Great Adventure', which promised that the paper would be 'the nation talking to itself' and would 'banish boredom from debate on public affairs,' ran three of the most pedestrian and worst-written articles ever set in type. The interests and aspirations of youth were to be reflected by three writers whose aggregate age was well over 200 years: 'A Sentimental Shoogle Down Memory Lane,' by John McShane — twenty paragraphs on Glasgow tramcars which disappeared more than fifteen years beforehand; 'It's Time at Least to Talk Gardening,' by Church of Scotland minister James L. Dow, and an article by Harry Pirie, a retired Glasgow sheriff, headlined 'Let's Give the Police these Extra Powers to Beat the Thugs.' The legal expert argued that police should be given stop-and-search powers to examine people suspected of being in possession of offensive weapons. The Chicago-style vision of suspects, arms and legs splayed against the walls (the paper used just such a picture alongside), had already been proposed in a report under the chairmanship of Court of Session Judge Lord Hunter. One member of the committee had dissociated himself from their conclusions on the grounds that the proposed powers were an infringement of individual liberty and raised a danger of police abuse.

It's worth a mention [wrote Pirie dismissively] that the professor who'd have no part in the proposal was not a lawyer, though lawyers have been battling for ages with the thorny problem of balancing public interest against individual liberty.

There's nothing wrong with the present Act (the

100

Prevention of Crime Act, 1953) except that it doesn't work and can never work effectively until the police are given the power to do the job.

In that first dummy there was no sign of the much-heralded investigative journalism, not even a stimulating news selection to surprise the reader. Graphically, it was a nightmare. 'We were battling with old types left over from Beaverbrook,' chief sub-editor Rusty Steele recalled, 'and with sub-editors mainly in the same category.' The other five dummies before the launch showed no great improvement. There was, therefore, nothing in the brief gestation period to suggest that the coming birth would produce a new kind of newspaper.

On Wednesday, April 30, Nathan Goldberg took over Saxton's foreign page and overlapped Pages 2 and 3 to produce a graphic picture-special on Vietnam, headed 'A City Burns as Yanks Go Home!'. The front page carried thirty inches of headline space with the legend 'Bring Him Back' and a long story on the endless travails of John Stonehouse. Another twenty inches of the front page were taken up with a picture of Prince Charles in a pit helmet.

Featured prominently on an inside page was the paper's imitable female columnist Dorothy-Grace Elder. Modelling her style on the *Daily Express*'s Jean Rook, Dorothy-Grace specialised in double-barrelled attacks on public personalities from Sir Alec Douglas (now Lord) Home to the Bay City Rollers. Hers was the 'So . . .' style of journalism. Thus in Wednesday's dummy, two of her six vignettes began in this way — 'So John Fairfax is at it again,' and 'So the invasion of Scotland is on.' Her lead bitch piece was titled 'Why Must Jackie Look So Damned Ordinary on a £4,000 Binge?' a reference to the hard-up Jackie Onassis selling off her old clothes to buy new.

Friday's dummy splashed a horrific murder and rape trial involving a man who claimed to be involved with the Ulster Defence Association. 'Life For The Beast of Belfast' trumpeted the paper over thirty-eight inches, and alongside it carried a large picture of the murderer and an accomplice.

The leader page was dominated by a photograph of a Scottish landscape alongside a flattering profile of the chief executive of the Scottish Tourist Board. Below this came a masterpiece of obscurity and irrelevance, 'Barrel Bungs Come to an End Down at the Old Spurtle Mill.'

By the end of the pre-launch week there were simmering rows on the production floors about the unpromising content of the paper. The 'inkies' downstairs had done their job. They had proved in the dummy runs that they could produce an excellently printed letterpress broadsheet in less time and with fewer men than in the Beaverbrook regime. They felt that the journalists had let them down by failing to find a vivid new style. This was certainly true. But there were constraints on the journalists which were, perhaps, not appreciated on the lower floors. The lack of stimulus and direction from the editorial chair was not understood anywhere other than among the journalists, and the shortage of staff, especially in the newsroom, was crippling any attempt at long-term investigations.

Andrew McCallum, a former reporter and sub-editor with Beaverbrook, had been appointed news editor. He had just over a dozen reporters in Glasgow to bring in the bulk of the news for the sixteen-page newspaper. And in the week prior to the launch they were concentrating on finding stories for the real paper. McCallum had a robust manner which upset some of his staff, but his will and his capacity for work were respected. But, like the other department heads, his news vision had been blinkered by his years with Beaverbrook so that he was myopic to everything except fire engines, ambulances and police cars.

To cover the rest of Scotland McCallum had, by launch day, only two other offices comprising five reporters. Three were based in Edinburgh and two in Aberdeen. There were no photographers and not even a picture wire to send prints to Albion Street. It was an impossible situation. There were to be five editions each night of the *Scottish Daily News* — Aberdeen and the North, Dundee, Edinburgh, Lanark and Glasgow — and the news editor had at his disposal fewer reporters for the whole country than the 'quality' papers like the *Glasgow Herald* and the *Scotsman*. And in two of his edition areas he did not even have a staff man. For national news McCallum had a three-man team operating from a cramped office off Fleet Street and serviced by only one telephone. Of the three, one was permanently at the House of Commons; the second, Ted Whitehead, was hardly prolific, which left one man, Tim Gopsill, to cover most of the national news and to work up the occasional investigative article.

The staffing projection for the editorial departments — reporters, sub-editors, features and sport — had been ninety, including the regional offices. But by launch day on May 5 there were only seventy-five journalists on the paper. There were two reasons for this shortfall. The first was that several people who were committed to joining the *Daily News* were still under contract to other organisations; but, more important, the *Daily News* rate of pay, at £69 a week*, was substantially less than the going rate for national daily journalists in Scotland and they were not offering the same level of perks, which range from car allowances, telephone and secretarial expenses to newspaper allowances and appearance money. Thus the ordinary rank-and-file journalist on a rival newspaper had no financial incentive to move to what might be short-lived and underpaid employment. So the journalists on the *News* fell into three separate categories; the bulk who had worked for the *Daily Express* or *Citizen* for a number of years, most of whom could not find other jobs, the raw recruits who had little or no daily newspaper experience, and those who had come out of a genuine feeling for the ideals involved.

One journalist who felt strongly attracted to the workers' newspaper which was being fashioned in Glasgow was Mary Holland, a former columnist of the *Observer*, now a presenter of the ITV current affairs programme 'Weekend World.' Ms Holland had been approached to become deputy editor which, had she accepted, would have put an end to the hopes Goldberg and Macgee harboured for the editor's chair. Ten days before the launch she travelled to Albion Street to discuss the job with the editorial executives and journalists. The approach to her had come, initially, from the promptings on the Works Council of Allister Mackie who saw in her progressive ideals he felt the paper should be striving to express. She was a talented, lucid writer, with wide experience and contacts, possessing a distinctive vision of what newspapers might be.

---

*Journalists on the *Scottish Daily News* were paid a basic £69 a week, but there were a number of special categories earning more, up to £150 a week for the Editor.

The third floor at Albion Street, the editorial, resembles every other journalistic receiving ward in the country; grimy, hosed down in dredge colour — cadaver grey, sewage blue — big as a cricket field and as barren, with occasional pillars keeping apart the concrete slabs. There are few interior walls — to call it open-plan would be a grotesque misdescription — only flimsy tin partitions here and there to mark off the library, the copy takers, the wire room, the darkroom and two filing drawer offices for the editor and managing editor to retreat from the bedlam outside. The ceiling of the department is tangled with the intestines of the building, fluorescent lights, steam and water pipes, electric conduits, extractor ducts and suction tubes down which metal containers stuffed with subbed copy whistle and clank.

Mary Holland emerged from one of the two offices with Fred Sillitto, Nathan Goldberg and Ray Chard, the managing editor, to meet some of the journalists she was considering joining. A knot of about thirty gathered in a half-circle facing her and Sillitto. She explained that she had been asked to join the paper, that she had a great deal of sympathy with the concept, but that there were practical and personal problems she had to consider — the uprooting of her children, for instance.

The journalists began to ask questions, led by features editor Alastair Wilson, his deputy Iain Campbell and sports sub-editor Harry Houston. The atmosphere was strained. The questioners were trying to expunge the presence of Mary Holland with a series of questions underlaid with bitter hostility, implicitly challenging her journalistic integrity. Her coverage of Northern Ireland was brought up; she was accused of favouring the Catholics, of being sympathetic to the IRA and of not giving the Protestant side of the issues. Why had she left the *Observer*? Was it not because the management felt her writings were unbalanced? Ms Holland answered the questions fully and reasonably, even the grossest from Harry Houston, 'Would we be able to sell our paper to an Orangeman in Bridgeton if you were writing for it?'

Some of the journalists were sickened by the baiting and worrying but they did nothing to stop it. At one point Ms Holland sat down on the desk which was covered with a greasy patina. She left the meeting with a broad stain on the back of her skirt. She did not come back.

The first issue of the *Scottish Daily News* appeared in a blaze of publicity. The front page splash 'It's Great to be Alive' — was a human interest story about a girl who had been dead on arrival at a Glasgow hospital after a car crash but had revived and eventually began a career as a model. The accompanying story — 'And that goes for us too' — introduced the worker-controlled paper to the reading public. Page 3 gave more of the same, half of it devoted to a photo-spread of the launch. Headlined 'Up, up and we're away,' the two large pictures showed a hot-air balloon, bedecked with *Daily News* regalia, taking off from a city park, and Tony Benn, Allister Mackie and Robert Maxwell — 'the unholiest trinity', as one sub-editor wanted the caption — shaking hands and smiling toothy smiles at the camera.

The political polarisation of the editorial was apparent in the first issue. On the front page there was a double-column story, headlined 'Your Majesty is no Comrade,' which began: 'The miners of South Wales are in no doubt who broke the Social Contract. Their annual report points the finger quite definitely at the lady who holds court at Buckingham Palace.' But, over the page, under the headline 'Reds Emptied City,' an agency story told of the forced evacuation of the population of the Cambodian capital, Phnom Penh, by the victorious Communist Khmer Rouge army.

The leader page was devoted to more self-congratulation. Andrew McCallum, the news editor, 'looked back without anger' at the thirteen-month struggle to launch the paper under the headline 'It was a Battle all the Way.'

On the same page a five-column cartoon showed two hands shaking with the *Daily News* building in the background. One hand came from a pin-striped suit, the other was bare and brawny: the legend was 'We're all on the SAME side now.'

Page 11 took the political pendulum back to the left with a half page by the excellent political editor Andrew Hargrave bringing the paper out against Britain's entry into the Common Market. Dorothy-Grace Elder exposed her claws on Page 13 with an attack on the state visit of Japanese

Emperor Hirohito to Britain — 'The ex-King of Heaven deserves a kick up the kimono not a State visit.'

Tuesday's paper underlined the inconsistent political approach with the threatened cut-back of Scottish steel jobs — 'You're Not On Monty' — and a Page 2 lead entitled 'Haven for Heroes', about 500 South Vietnamese soldiers who had arrived at the US base on Guam after fleeing from the Vietcong. Page 3 carried a huge picture story about a young mother who had taken up stripping to boost the family budget and the leader page featured the infamous 'Spurtle Mill' feature by Iain Campbell, though with a marginally less obscure title.

By Wednesday of the first week the political balance was firmly to the left, as the paper reported moves to force Sir Monty Finniston to resign from the chairmanship of the British Steel Corporation, and led on an investigation into allegations that North Sea divers were at risk because firms were refusing to release information on new research into their safety. The leader page was now settling into a rut of trivial tourist-type features with a story on ghosts in Scottish castles and the uncritical profile of the Scottish Tourist Board which had appeared in the first dummy newspaper.

Thursday and Friday saw the paper keep up the same political/industrial coverage with reports on Tony Benn's attempts to hold on to his position as Industry Secretary and Chrysler's 'suspect' plan to involve workers in the management of the car company. Friday's front page was particularly striking, carrying on the top left a photograph of 'bread queues in the land of milk and honey,' showing hundreds of South Vietnamese refugees queuing for food at an army camp in Southern California. Friday's paper also featured the first contribution from Tory MP Teddy Taylor alongside Labour's Norman Buchan, in the 'Open Forum' section. Four days earlier, viewers to Granada's 'World in Action' had watched a fierce attack on Fred Sillitto by works councillors Jimmy McNamara and Charlie Armstrong over the plan to allow Taylor to contribute to the *Daily News*.

The second week of publication began with the circulation, which had peaked at 330,000 on the third day, falling away. This had been foreseen, losing readers who had bought the *Daily News* for a few days out of curiosity and then returned to their normal newspaper. What was not perceived at this stage was the deep dissatisfaction with the new paper, which would see the circulation graph plunge inexorably until after the *Daily News* had been relaunched as a tabloid newspaper.

The odd mixture of 'human interest' stories, dull features, with industrial coverage and major news items angled to the left continued. Thursday's late editions of the paper, like every other paper in the country, carried reports of the US Marines' action to recover the freighter Mayaguez, held in the Gulf of Thailand by Cambodian warships. But the *Daily News* differed from its rivals in the way it handled the story. In the second-last edition of the night, under a prominent picture of President Ford smiling broadly into the camera, a headline said, 'No time for laughing as US sinks three boats guarding captive ship.' And the final edition, with the same photograph, accused Ford of 'taking the war back to South-east Asia,' as the headline reported the 2 a.m. news of US Marines releasing the imprisoned ship.

Friday's paper followed up with a photograph of Ford, Kissinger and other administration members grouped round a desk in the White House, convulsed with laughter. The day's front page splash was a story by Industrial Editor James Fyfe on lay-offs at the troubled Chrysler plant at Linwood. On Saturday the *News* described the US action as 'The rescue that never was . . . and it cost 14 men.'

One characteristic of the *Scottish Daily News* which was consistent throughout the first two weeks was the way that it changed, visibly and politically, with the different editions during the night.

The first edition, for the North of Scotland, was presided over by Fred Sillitto who usually left with the first edition at 10 p.m. Nathan Goldberg, night editor Jack Wills, and John Hodgman took the paper through until the morning, usually gutting and remaking the front page for the second and succeeding editions which served the greater part of the circulation area.

The presentation of the news was overtly political during this period and, depending on the political sympathies of the reader, this was seen either as courageous objectivity or blatant distortion. But to potential advertisers, on whom the newspaper depended for about half its revenue, the selection and treatment of news seemed biased in favour of trade unions in its heavy industrial coverage and against big business, the free enterprise system in general and against its epicentre, the United States.

Eric Tough, the general manager brought in from PA Management Consultants Ltd, recalled the reaction of potential advertisers:

'I offered free half-pages to major advertisers. And the reaction was "If I want to kill my bloody product I'll advertise in your newspaper." We gained a reputation very fast. In our first six weeks we had nine dud front pages. Highly emotive, left-wing front pages. And then the Ladbroke's thing. That killed us, crucified us. Two national advertisers phoned me and said that their industries were extremely sensitive to strikes. One said, "If your newspaper is going to back strikers just because they're strikers then the sooner your paper's dead the better. I'm not going to keep alive a newspaper which, the first time I get a strike, will back the strikers irrespective of my problems."'

The *Daily News* had been carrying on a front-page campaign for 300 West of Scotland betting shop workers sacked by Ladbrokes when they went on strike for union recognition. One photograph showed a group of employees brought in from England by the company: the flying strike-breakers they were called by the *SDN*, which prompted Ladbrokes to issue a writ.

'I was continually trying to tell the *Daily News* board (the Works Council plus two outside investors, the general manager and the editor) that the balancing factor was advertising' [Tough said] 'You must remember that you must write newspapers not just to get circulation but to get advertising. I don't believe there was any bias against the newspaper from advertisers — they'll advertise in any paper that's going to get them sales. They said, "We suspect what's going to happen, we know you're full of communists but we're prepared to see a good paper and if it is we'll advertise. But if you're going to have the thing run by the handful of guys who pushed Beaverbrook into the ditch then you've had it."

'Dougie Ferguson, the circulation manager, would come to me either almost in tears or screeching blind fury because he had to sell the paper. "Look at it," he'd say, showing me yesterday's paper. "How can I try to sell a paper like that?" Jimmy Galt, the advertising manager, would come in with his head in his hands saying, "I'm frightened to phone agencies to try to get adverts." The three of us sat day after day in that office of mine talking that way. And we'd tackle Nat Goldberg or wee Jimmy McNamara and say, "You know, this is commercial, it's not for fun, it isn't for kicks. You're not selling this paper to readers only you're selling it to advertisers too!"

'And Jimmy McNamara would say, "Well Eric, if it comes to principle or profit I know which we'll choose every time." '

The largest-selling newspaper in Scotland, the IPC-owned *Daily Record*, also had a claimed left-of-centre standpoint but had little difficulty in attracting advertising.

'Advertisers saw the *Daily Record* as a much more responsible paper, it had a management therefore it had people who breathe the same kind of air as other managers. So they trusted it not to go too far. They could talk to the management over lunch in the right kind of clubs. They had no idea what the hell we would do when Nat Goldberg went off on one of his wilder communistic flights of fancy. They just didn't trust us.'

Allied to the distrust with which advertisers viewed the *Daily News* was the dissatisfaction felt by a large part of the readership. From a peak of 330,000 the paper was slipping down a seemingly bottomless circulation slope — at below 200,000 by the end of the third week. It was evident that the lumpy mix of industrial splashes, bland features and salacious crime (MY ORDEAL AT THE HANDS OF A BACKSTREET ABORTIONIST; SCHOOLGIRLS CAUGHT IN VICE TRAP; SALIVA CLUE TO RAPIST — all from Page 5, Tuesday, May 20) was turning off readers at a rate of more than 10,000 a day. Against this background Maxwell sent his voluminous telex which prophesied early demise if he was not recalled: but his time hadn't yet come.

8

Robert Maxwell

In his library at Headington Hill Hall, Oxford, Robert Maxwell has a special set of leather-bound volumes. They bear the name of no author, no publisher, just two gold-plated words — 'Robert Maxwell'. Between the opulent covers lies the public record of the achievements and disasters in the fifty-two-year life of a remarkable man.

Robert Maxwell is not unique in being preoccupied with his public image. But the lengths to which he will go to make a reality of that image are extraordinary. What else could take a man from being the youngest of six children of a peasant family in Slovakia to chief executive of the first workers' co-operative newspaper in Britain.

Many people directly or indirectly involved in the *Scottish Daily News* found themselves asking, time and again, 'Why's he doing it? What's in it for him?' as each new Maxwell tactic failed to fit into a cogent pattern. It is difficult — and can be dangerous — to speculate on a person's motives and both the difficulty and the danger are intense in the case of Robert Maxwell.

In public his motives were simple. He was asked by a group of determined Scottish newspaper workers to help them save their jobs and, being a good Socialist and a successful businessman, he felt bound to offer to help and advise. But one thing Robert Maxwell is not is a simple man.

He was, as is well known, born Jan Ludwig Hoch. During the Second World War he used the names Jones and Du Maurier and finally settled on Maxwell; the name first came to the attention of the publishing world when he cornered the market in captured German scientific documents after the war. He acquired the documents from

110

the notorious German publisher Julius Springer (whose *Bild Zeitung* makes the *Daily Mirror* look like a serious literary magazine). The information in the documents was of such technical and scientific importance that libraries throughout the Western World were soon falling over each other to pay the grossly inflated prices being charged by the young entrepreneur, who had now settled in England.

This money-making technique laid the foundations for the whole Pergamon empire as it grew over the next two decades — buy up scientific and technical talent, corner the market and charge libraries high prices for the information. But before Pergamon came into existence Maxwell spent three years failing to rescue the ailing book wholesaling firm Simkin Marshall. It finally went bankrupt with debts of £475,000, and Maxwell had made himself widely unpopular in the refined world of publishing for his abrasive business manner.

He had further commercial disasters to come, but Pergamon Press blossomed in the lush grounds of Headington Hill Hall. Maxwell had moved into the great mansion as a step, so many people thought, towards acquiring the image of a respectable member of the Establishment. But even that analysis of his motives is too simple because a respectable member of the English Establishment does not enter politics under the flag of the Labour Party, however pale pink that flag may have become.

Buckingham is hardly a rock-solid Labour stronghold, but Maxwell won the seat in the 1964 General Election and probably ruined his prospects of a political career on his first day in the House of Commons. He pushed too hard and too soon. He used a procedural device to speak for twenty minutes, delayed an important foreign affairs speech by Harold Wilson and thereby deprived the Prime Minister of his anticipated coverage in the evening papers.

In the late 1960s Robert Maxwell's world started to fall in on top of him. In September 1968 he failed in a £26m bid to take control of the *News of the World* organisation, beaten by Australian publisher Rupert Murdoch. In the following year negotiations between Pergamon and the American Leasco Data Processing Corporation broke down at the last minute when Leasco began to have doubts about

111

the glowing profit forecasts made by Maxwell about his company.

The aborted takeover led to an investigation by the Department of Trade and Industry and, to cut a very long and complex story short, the report concluded that Robert Maxwell was 'not a person who can be relied on to exercise proper stewardship of a publicly quoted company.' It might have damned Maxwell for ever, but its contents were never given widespread publicity because Maxwell immediately slapped writs on the Department and its inspectors, effectively inhibiting public mention of the report. Free quotation of the inspectors' findings only became possible in April 1974 when the House of Lords contemptuously threw out Maxwell's action to suppress the report.

And to complete a disastrous two years, in 1970 Robert Maxwell lost his Buckingham seat and the coveted initials MP after his name. A man with less energy and belief in his own destiny might have been destroyed by any one of these setbacks. Robert Maxwell not only survived but survived unscathed.

He fought to resume control of Pergamon in 1974. And if he abandoned all hopes of picking up the pieces of his political career he still had active ambitions to own a newspaper business. And the *Scottish Daily News* presented him with an opportunity of realising that ambition and even restoring something of his damaged political image.

All the information, and more, required to make a reasonably accurate assessment of Robert Maxwell as a businessman has existed, in public, for several years. But the information had never been presented in a form or through a medium which would have brought it to the notice of the workforce of the *Scottish Daily News*. Most people had a rather vague impression of a millionaire Socialist, determined, energetic and fiercely patriotic about his adopted country. It was not at all a bad pedigree to bring into an enterprise like the *Scottish Daily News* and, despite the warning hints they had from trade union officials and civil servants, the workforce can hardly be blamed for accepting Maxwell's money and advice in the dark days of 1974 when the world seemed full of people ready to throw large quantities of cold water over the faint spark of hope that kept them going.

But the Department of Trade and Industry knew what

Maxwell was like, and it should not have taken a great leap of the imagination for civil servants and politicians involved to predict what effect Robert Maxwell would have on a flickering workers' co-operative enterprise.

Professor Richard Briston had been invited, by Maxwell, to act as financial adviser to the *Scottish Daily News* before the paper was launched. Briston's early anxieties about Maxwell's involvement were reinforced by what he saw of the millionaire's tactics when things started to go wrong. But Briston has no doubts where the major share of the blame for the situation should lie:

'I think the role of the Government has been a very bad influence. The Government made it so difficult for the workers to raise the necessary money that they almost imposed a financial straitjacket on the enterprise. They created a situation where the workers had to go public, where they had to invest their own money, where they had to accept Mr Maxwell's money.

'Now, in the light of what the DTI had uncovered from its investigations into Mr Maxwell's managerial style, they, I would argue, are responsible for creating the situation. All the Government had to do was to put in the extra £114,000 and the newspaper could have started as a complete co-operative.'

But the workers had to accept Maxwell's money and, if some of the leaders of the co-operative hoped they could take his money and then get rid of him, they found out, too late, about the man's drive, determination and irrepressible appetite for manipulation and intrigue. If they had known, or had been told, something of his past dealings they might have realised that a toe-hold is an adequate base from which Robert Maxwell can climb back up to the top of the cliff.

The Executive Council of the *Scottish Daily News* met on April 16 to strip Robert Maxwell of all his positions in the company. At a mass meeting of the workforce on April 17 the workforce accepted the executive decision with the qualification that Maxwell should be allowed to retain his co-chairmanship of the Executive Council. It was a title without substance and it was offered in a spirit of guilt at the idea of throwing the man out altogether when he had, after all, given a fair amount of time and money to the enterprise. The Executive Council had to accept the amendment to their recommendation but they still reckoned they had effectively banished Maxwell from the organisation and would be free to continue the project without his disruptions. They reckoned without Maxwell's ability to see a half-chance and seize it. The man they thought they had thrown over the edge into oblivion was, in reality, clinging out of sight waiting for the moment to reappear.

In mid-April, then, Maxwell was out of sight. By the beginning of June — just six weeks later — he had been voted back on to the Executive Council by the workforce. It was an extraordinary recovery, even by Maxwell's standards, and it was achieved through his clever handling of a panic-stricken workforce.

Within four weeks of the launch of the newspaper it was clear that the *Scottish Daily News* was suffering from a disastrous combination of steadily falling sales and a persistent lack of advertising. The workers faced the prospect of losing the money they had invested in the enterprise — around £500 to £600 each — and, much more seriously, they were once again haunted by the spectre of unemployment. Maxwell told them, frequently, forcefully and convincingly, that he and he alone could save the enterprise. If he failed to convince all of them that this was so, he convinced enough of them that there was something in what he was saying to win a seat on the executive at the mass meeting of June 4. True, he scraped home by just seven votes, but it gave him a handhold to add to his toehold and it gave him the new and bizarre position of being a 'shop-floor representative'. When the constitution of the company had been drawn up the idea of having shop-floor representatives on the Executive Council had been simple enough. In the terms of the workers' co-operative it was to ensure that the rank-and-file had a dominant voice on the decision-making body. The idea had been that the workers themselves would fill these positions. Maxwell had, however, interpreted the phrase to mean a person elected *by* the shop-floor workers who need not be *from* the shop floor. It was an interpretation which, though it made a nonsense of the original intention, was not actually inadmissable.

The elections of June 4 were strange in other ways. The original Executive Council had been elected by the members of the Action Committee which had run the

114

thirteen-month campaign to launch the paper. But they had naïvely forgotten that under the constitution of Scottish News Enterprises, the first Annual General Meeting had to be held within one year of the incorporation of the company. The year ended on June 5 so that, at a critical and difficult moment just a month after the paper had been launched, almost the entire Executive Council had to offer themselves for re-election by the workforce.

Robert Maxwell resigned as co-chairman of the executive and had not submitted a nomination for the election, but when the mass meeting was under way he insisted that nominations from the floor of the meeting should be acceptable. The existing executive councillors argued that this procedure was not permitted under the constitution but they were overruled. And the already bemused workers became utterly baffled when the election mechanism was revealed.

When the votes for and against were finally counted the result was that two of the original Executive Council — James McNamara and Charlie Armstrong — had failed to be re-elected. In their places were Robert Maxwell and Nathan Goldberg. Maxwell was back by just seven votes.

He had, quite simply, out-thought and out-manoeuvred his opponents; he had confirmed his ability to swing a mass meeting by his oratory and he now knew that he had a dependable support amongst the workforce which would be his base for consolidating and expanding his role in the organisation.

Robert Maxwell is an impressive figure. He is large and fierce and clearly a man who has discovered from experience that people will do what you tell them to do, if you tell them the right way. He stands head and shoulders above the crowd, not only physically but, more significantly, in the drive that he brings to everything that he does. Most people cannot compete with him, either because they are daunted by his speed of thought or because they lack his energy at turning thought into action. The most absurd feat of imagination would be to think of Robert Maxwell sitting on a sunny bank by the side of a limpid pool idly chewing a blade of grass. He would have the river dammed, its water sold off and the grass reaped to make paper while the rest of humanity watched in bemusement.

115

The Action Committee members who visited Maxwell at Oxford came away with schizophrenic feelings. They would sit in one of his huge and opulently furnished baronial rooms, drinking from a perfectly matched monogrammed tea service (except that Maxwell's cup was larger than anyone else's) despising themselves for being attracted to the rotund talisman in front of them.

So long as the commercial prospects of the *Scottish Daily News* grew bleaker, Robert Maxwell's claim to be the only possible saviour grew stronger. He argued that he, and he alone, could revitalise the advertising situation through his business acumen and his extensive contacts among potential advertisers. And he, and he alone, could push up circulation and bring to the enterprise an air of success and commercial viability.

It was a stark choice for the workforce. Either they accepted Maxwell's claims and threw themselves behind his strategy or they faced up to the growing evidence that the paper, as a co-operative enterprise, was going to fail. A job with Maxwell, or the dole with dignity. And, paradoxically, the very democratic structure of the enterprise was Maxwell's strongest card. With the June 4 election result to reassure him, Maxwell knew that he could go directly to the workforce through the device of mass meetings and, by presenting the issue in stark terms, guarantee himself a majority of supporters at the meeting.

Professor Richard Briston explains the technique:

'One of the weaknesses of the co-operative system is that, if a person has the strength of mind and the oratorial ability to appeal to so-called democratic processes, then he can very often win the day. If, for example, a vote goes against you in the Executive Council, you can say, "All right, I abide by that vote but I feel it should be put to a mass meeting of the workers because, after all, we are a co-operative." And then, if you can present the issues the right way, you will get the vote reversed.'

A variation of the technique, also used by Maxwell, is to reintroduce the subject of contrary votes at sparsely attended meetings of the executive. One of the best and, in the long term, most significant examples of this method is outlined by

116

Iain Bain, former financial controller of the *Scottish Daily News*.

'At that meeting Robert Maxwell proposed that he be vested with responsibility for advertising and circulation. Now the next meeting of the Executive Council was set for the following week, but the very next morning Robert Maxwell called an emergency meeting of the Executive Council for that afternoon. Naturally the meeting was sparsely attended — only five of the ten members were there.

'At that meeting Robert Maxwell proposed that the price of the paper should be reduced from 6p to 5p. Now this idea had already been discussed by the council in June and had been firmly rejected, but at this emergency meeting the decision was reversed. I was given a chance to voice my opinion but, of course, it had no effect.'

Robert Maxwell, unsurprisingly, has a different interpretation of these events. He admitted publicly that the decision to drop the price was his own decision. But he added: 'I'm the manager and the workers have invested me with executive powers. I felt that we needed, in order to be sure of our viability in the market place, that the price go to 5p and I took that decision. But being a democrat I took it to the Executive Council, the Executive Council approved it and I therefore acted totally constitutionally within the procedures laid down in the workers' co-operative.'

It is worth looking in some detail later at this decision to lower the price because, according to the best commercial opinion on the subject, it was a disastrous decision for the *Scottish Daily News*. If that is so then Maxwell's claims that he was the 'saviour' of the newspaper ring hollow, and his commercial judgment, as well as his management style, undermined the chances of success of the project.

But the Maxwells of this world win if they keep on the move. The trail of bitter enemies he leaves behind sooner or later set off in pursuit: angry people find the energy and weapons to take him on.

In the *Scottish Daily News* — as in his other enterprises, according to the Department of Trade report — Maxwell insisted on total, unquestioning loyalty from his executives as from all his workers, and refused to concede even the possibility that anything he did could be wrong. Within six weeks of him taking office as Chief Executive, all of the executives and professional advisers brought in from outside had resigned. Eric Tough resigned as general manager; Iain Bain resigned as financial controller; Rankin Durnin took over but soon resigned; Richard Briston resigned as financial adviser; William Wolfe, chairman of the Scottish National Party and a professional accountant, resigned as company secretary; French and Cowan, a large firm of accountants, withdrew as auditors. And the main cause of the resignations was, predictably, that they found it impossible to work with Robert Maxwell.

Two weeks or so after the relaunch of the *Scottish Daily News* in tabloid form (which will be looked at more widely in the next chapter), circulation had settled — at last — at around 150,000 copies a day. For the first time since the paper started sales figures had levelled out and it was reasonable to suppose that circulation would stay at that level, provided the quality of the newspaper did not deteriorate, and might well rise if the quality of the content could be improved.

Market research, carried out by System Three (Scotland), had shown clearly that readers' outstanding objection to the first version of the *Scottish Daily News* was its size. Price, layout, content and all the other factors suggested by the market researchers were insignificant in readers' (or former readers') estimation of the newspaper.

The obvious conclusion from this was that readers were quite content to pay 6p for the newspaper (indeed the fact that the *Daily News* did not gain a single reader when its tabloid rival the *Daily Record* increased to 6p supports this), and this is the conclusion the Executive Council came to at their meeting of July when the proposal to reduce the price to 5p was first brought up.

Indeed, it was arguable that the *Scottish Daily News*, with higher reader loyalty than usual because of the nature of the enterprise, might even sell at a penny or two above the price of its rivals without losing sales.

Robert Maxwell was unimpressed by this line of reasoning. The paper needed a sales gimmick, he argued, and in these inflationary times what better gimmick than to *lower* the price and present to the public the image of a newspaper fighting inflation in a practical way. And that is exactly how it was presented. He was sure that a cut of one-sixth in price would be offset by an increase of one-sixth in sales. Unhappily, that is not the way newspaper finances operate. In order to bring in the same revenue from sales at 5p as had come in from a 6p cover price, the newspaper had to sell not one-sixth more copies (that is raising circulation from 150,000 to 175,000), but nearly *three times* as many copies. So the decision to drop the to 5p not only ran counter to all the market research evidence, it imposed an almost impossible task of raising circulation by 300%.

Assuming, therefore, that sales would have remained about the same whether the price was 5p or 6p — an assumption which Maxwell would reject — the financial position of the *Scottish Daily News* would have changed dramatically after the relaunch. At 5p the paper was, in fact, losing about £17,000 a week; at 6p that fatal drain on the cash reserves would have been cut to about £8,000. At worst that would have delayed the final cash crisis by nearly six months. At best, that time could have been used to improve content and boost sales, search out more advertising and, possibly, find new cash to bridge the gap until income could be increased. Now that might not have happened, the newspaper might just have died later rather than sooner. But it is clear that the only realistic hope of saving the *Scottish Daily News* was to hold the price at 6p — or increase it — and, therefore, if one decision can be identified as the final fatal mistake it was Maxwell's decision to lower the price.

This view of the financial situation is confirmed — as indeed it was at the time — by Eric Tough, Richard Briston and Iain Bain. Only Robert Maxwell and his supporters on the Executive Council believed there was any sense in the decision to lower the price; but their opinion was the one that counted in the end and, whatever doubts the workforce might have had about the decision, they agreed to Maxwell's whole package of strategies. By mid-September the great majority of the workers had been persuaded that they had just two choices — inevitable liquidation under the old Allister Mackie regime or a chance of success by accepting everything proposed by Robert Maxwell. Now, with hindsight, it is clear that the reality was almost exactly the opposite: barring a miracle, liquidation was inevitable at the price set by Maxwell, while there was at least a tangible hope if the price could be restored to 6p.

Eric Tough, the general manager, resigned after Maxwell won unconditional support from the workforce:

'Now I think we were so undercapitalised that we couldn't have made it anyway. But we might have been able to go to the Government and say that we were doing better and to plead for more money and more time to sort these things out. The paper did, after all, improve tremendously. But having got mixed up with Maxwell and with these emotional, non-commercial considerations, the Government was bound to say "No".'

Criticising Robert Maxwell is a very perilous activity, as two Department of Trade inspectors realised when he sued them. But one thing at least can be said with utter confidence — the intervention of Maxwell in the *Scottish Daily News* effectively ruined the project as a test-bed for new industrial relations in the newspaper industry, or in industry in general. Leaving aside the question of whether his commercial decisions were wrong or his management style incompatible with a workers' co-operative, Maxwell introduced an unknown, unquantifiable factor into the situation and, for good or ill, his presence so smudged the attempts by the workers themselves to run their own newspaper that no conclusions can be drawn from the experiment which can be applied with confidence elsewhere.

It is, of course, unfair to blame Maxwell for this effect of his presence. The opportunity presented itself and, in his own terms, Maxwell made the most of it. Undoubtedly he believed that he was working for the ultimate good of the workforce. But here we should return to Professor Briston's accusation that the blame lies with the Government for allowing the project to go ahead but failing to ensure that it could be freed of the presence of Robert Maxwell.

Eric Tough also underlined this aspect when he expressed his disappointment that the clarity of the experiment was clouded by the presence of Maxwell. Tough had joined the project, full of doubts about its viability, but convinced of its value as an experiment. Not that he saw workers' control as an alternative to the capitalist system; on the contrary, Tough has never disguised the fact that he is a Tory and believes utterly that the best way of running society is on the basis of free enterprise. But he did see a possibility that workers' control might provide a solution in situations where a company is viable, but a breakdown in labour-management relations has brought on a crisis. Despite dire warnings from his business colleagues and friends that he was committing professional suicide by associating with the project, he wanted to play a part in the experiment and believed that the newspaper had a tangible, if remote, chance of success.

'My deep regret is that Maxwell crossed this whole field and ruined the possibility of this terribly vital experiment being taken to a satisfactory conclusion, one way or the other. We have no real idea now what might have been achieved and we can't even point to clear-cut reasons why things went wrong. Maxwell's presence, his influence, penetrated every issue.'

Perhaps the *Scottish Daily News* would have collapsed anyway. Perhaps the problems with editorial content, the management structure, and the persistent lack of cash reserves would never have been solved. Perhaps, for these and other reasons, workers' co-operatives can never work in the newspaper industry. But Robert Maxwell, through his very presence in Albion Street or in the background, ensured that no one will ever really know whether the *Scottish Daily News* could have been a successful experiment in workers' control.

9
The Relaunch

There was no euphoria at the relaunch of the *Scottish Daily News*, no champagne, no parade of celebrities. The workforce, for whom the threat of unemployment was looming again following the collapse of circulation and advertising, went into the Sunday night production routine on August 17 in a mood of sombre determination. Losses were running at £30,000 a week, a figure which, if continued, would see the paper buried in less than six months.

The decision to relaunch as a tabloid had been taken in July after a market survey had showed overwhelming preference among potential readers for a smaller paper, and after several trial runs outside normal production had proved that it was practicable to produce a tabloid on the modified presses.

The month before the August 18 relaunch had seen Robert Maxwell become chief executive of Scottish News Enterprises on the strength of a pledge to increase advertising and circulation. Circulation had shown no sign of bottoming out and was now running at 80,000 a day; advertising was less than 20% of a fourteen-page paper. The Maxwell solution to this twin blight was to cut the price of the relaunched paper to attract readers, backing this with a guaranteed rebate to advertisers on the *Daily News* page rate if circulation fell below 225,000. Maxwell, again on his own initiative, had begun to advertise in the broadsheet for expenses-paid volunteers to act as part-time circulation representatives to stimulate interest in the paper in their local areas by canvassing householders, shopkeepers and newsagents. This move was eventually dropped after an angry debate in the Federated Chapel: Robert Maxwell was accused by some of the FoCs of autocratically impinging, without consultation, on the jobs of regular circulation representatives employed by the newspaper.

The run-up period before the relaunch had also seen the appointment of Ralph Saunders, the editor of a weekly tabloid in Australia, to take charge of remodelling the *Daily News*, and his departure after three days, following an internal revolt.

Eric Tough, the general manager, was responsible for hiring the man:

'Fred Sillitto told me he had never produced a tabloid and lacked the necessary expertise. If you go from broadsheet to tabloid you can't just print yesterday's stories in today's tabloid. You need twice as many stories, half the length. No one had this particular experience. Fred agreed that we just had to get someone with the experience of managing a tabloid paper. There was, of course, an internal fight going on. Nathan Goldberg reckoned he could do it and one or two others supported him. Fred had grave doubts — he reckoned he could write for it but he couldn't run it. So he found a man who could, we thought.

'We got the man in, negotiated his salary and he turned up one Monday. By the Monday afternoon we had a deputation of the Executive Committee, led by Goldberg, saying, "You can't keep this guy, we're paying him too much." I said that there was a gap, we needed somebody and we were paying the market price (around £125 a week). Now everyone in the building was paying themselves substantially below the going rate and this was a problem I foresaw — the first time we were liable to lose someone out of the 500 who was unique, if you like, and replaced him from outside would we be big enough to pay him the going rate, despite the fact that they weren't paying themselves that kind of money. If they weren't prepared to do that then they weren't being commercial.

'The committee voted and Fred and I were instructed to go back and renegotiate this cut of about £30 a week in salary. I said, "But, look, you can't do this, engage people, give them a contract, have them leave their job and come to us and then tell them we've changed our minds, we're going to pay you £30 a week less." So we told the man, and he left the next day.'

Saunders had also run into flak from the graphic artists on the paper, especially over the only dummy he produced which, they felt, resembled something out of the Beaverbrook stable through its use of Century typefaces. At an editorial meeting the tabloid expert was candidly told by one of the artists, Albert Tonner, that the dummy 'just doesn't make it.' The art department, who considered themselves the arbiters of design and make-up, felt slighted by Saunders' appointment and when he failed to appear next day they took on the redesigning of the newspaper.

The artists drew up a number of dummy front pages using Letraset faces and finally decided to use a modern face, Franklin Gothic, as the main one. This required casting the typeface in metal from negatives of the rub-down lettering which, this time, was achieved without resistance from the process department — a measure of how desperation was affecting trade union practices. Only one dummy was printed with the new face and that was only a twelve-page paper without any real stories. And so the 500 *Scottish Daily News* workers went into the tabloid launch having never produced a truly simulated newspaper; the broadsheet was still being produced, and conversion of machinery and reorientation of staff had to be done concurrently, outside normal production hours.

Another problem which awaited the tabloid was the reluctance of newsagents to support it. The Newsagents' Federation had refused to advise their members to support the relaunch because the cover price, and therefore their profit margin, had been reduced by Robert Maxwell. In practice, this meant that newsagents would be less likely to display point-of-sale material or to push sales of the paper in any other way.

Neil Kidd, secretary of the Newsagents' Federation, explains:

'The position was that we made an arrangement with Mr Maxwell in regard to special terms when the price was, at that time, sixpence. And the very same day that arrangement came into being, he decided, by evening, to change it to fivepence.

124

'We were, quite frankly, flabbergasted. It's something unusual for us to make an arrangement in the morning and have it changed in the afternoon. We hope people, when we deal with them, put their cards on the table. There was no indication to us at all, no word that the cover price would change. He changed his mind at night, and that was that.'

This change of mind meant a reduction in newsagents' profit of 0.28p per copy. Their share of the cover price went down from 1.68p on a 6p paper to 1.40p on a 5p paper. The newsagents were not pleased. The *Scottish Daily Express* was giving them a higher percentage on a higher price, the *Daily Record* was giving higher commission and it would be increasing its price to 6p in the second week of the *Daily News'* relaunch. Moreover, for the first month, the *Scottish Daily News* would be on a sale or return basis, on the insistence of its distributors, which meant that newsagents could leave it under the counter, to push the competitors which they had to sell if they were not to lose money.

Robert Maxwell was now firmly in control of the *Scottish Daily News* as its chief executive, even though his authority had been specifically limited to advertising and circulation by a mass meeting on August 13. It had been his unilateral decision — subsequently endorsed by a badly attended Executive Council — to reduce the cover price. On his own initiative he had introduced the rebate to advertisers if circulation fell below 225,000. And by giving his guarantee to increase advertising and circulation he had the workforce eating out of his hand and had finally gained a dependable majority in his struggle with the Mackie faction in the Executive Council. The spectre of the dole and the reality of Maxwell's own commercial success had been an irresistible combination.

The print-run for the launch night on August 17 was 240,000. Backed up by a television and local radio advertising campaign, enhanced by news coverage in the media, the first edition of the remodelled *Scottish Daily News* came off the presses shortly before 10 p.m. There was no doubt that the appearance and size of the paper made it more marketable than the broadsheet, and a range of exclusive stories, written in a crisper style, caught readers' attention. But the features section, so important in a tabloid paper, had not risen above the mediocre. The paper was better — everyone agreed on that — but was it good enough?

There was still a debate going on about the price reduction. Allister Mackie, and those who agreed with his analysis, argued that any sales benefits were marginal with price reduction and were heavily outweighed by a sharp drop in revenue. Maxwell and his supporters claimed that the lower price was the main selling point and that circulation would blossom as a result, particularly as the *Daily Record* was soon adding 1p to its price, leaving the *Daily News* alone at 5p.

There was one calculation on which everyone agreed, that the paper had to gross £7,000 a day to meet fixed costs. This was the sum that Eric Tough had drummed into the consciousness of the workforce after the Maxwell telex in May, and it was never challenged. Maxwell held that this would be reached with a circulation of 250,000 (at £14 per 1,000 copies return to the company), along with nine pages of advertising (about 40% of the total pages) at £400 a page. Mackie challenged this optimism, saying that only present advertising ratios (that is, less than 20%) should be used in the calculation and, on that basis, circulation would have to be more than 600,000 with a 5p price.

Monday's paper was a sell-out, bringing a temporary resurgence of optimism to Albion Street. Sunday night's production had been enlivened by periodic Tannoy broadcasts from Maxwell reporting the progress of the paper, and on Monday he took this technique a stage further by giving a pep talk to the editorial department at 6 p.m., the peak point of their production schedule.

After complimenting the editorial staff on the first edition Maxwell reminded the assembled journalists that the paper had been late, missing the train to Edinburgh and, therefore, street sales in the capital. This would not be allowed to happpen under his regime, he told them. Edition times would be met 'even if we have to put out a paper with blank pages.'

By Wednesday, and a print run of 250,000, Robert Maxwell was saying that, while the newspaper was not out of its difficulties, 'we are extremely confident that things are going our way and that we have found the formula, a journalistic formula and a production formula, which will make this enterprise commercially viable and secure for many years to come.' Maxwell was also claiming 'a major breakthrough for the *Scottish Daily News*', referring to the fact that he personally had secured Government advertising covering twenty-five separate departments and bodies.

That same day Maxwell telephoned the Glasgow office of the Department of Trade and Industry: 'In line with our understanding of keeping the department informed of major developments I thought that you'd like to know that the paper has been a virtual sell-out. That really is a remarkable performance and it augurs well for the future. I don't want to give the impression that one swallow would make a summer, but that is a tremendous start.'

The terms of the Government loan required the newspaper to report, regularly, to the department. Maxwell, speaking slowly, almost gloatingly, went on: 'I'm sure you'll be as pleased as I am that the advertising interest has picked up very strongly indeed and, lastly, it appears that my decision — and it was mine — to go down to 5p will probably be very helpful to us because the *Daily Record* has decided to go up to 6p.

'The other point is that there is unanimity and all's well on the management side so we have no problems. And so, you know, the people here have got their tails right up.'

Maxwell's presence had infiltrated every cranny of the Albion Street building: he was to be seen on the production floors urging on the men, having a quiet word in the ear of the editor or back-bench subs and in the early hours of the morning he was even found frying himself hamburgers in the canteen kitchen.

He had commandeered a room on the fourth floor as sleeping quarters, although he was still registered at Glasgow's top hotel, the Albany. He was firing off commands without reference to the Executive Council, and he even told the Federated Chapel that he would not abide by any decision which he did not consider was in the best interests of the paper, whether it came from management, from the unions or both. Above all, he longed to destroy the last vestiges of power that remained with Allister Mackie.

Four days before the tabloid launch Maxwell had talked with Scottish Graphical Association FoC Joe McGowan, and members of his chapel, ostensibly to finalise arrangements for the relaunch. During the course of the conversation he let it be known that he could not make the 'necessary decisions relative to the survival of the paper', because he and Mackie could not work together: either Mackie must go or he would.

The Scottish Graphical Association in Beaverbrook were renowned as a right-wing and Protestant-orientated chapel. Most of the members, other workers would joke, were either Freemasons or Orangemen and the jobs in the caseroom were handed down with due reverence and nepotism; it was a case of 'the type my father set.' Allister Mackie had been FoC of the chapel and latterly Imperial Father of the Federated Chapel, but he was an aberration as a liberal Socialist. His own chapel had even passed a motion of no confidence in him as chairman of the Executive Council in the early stages of his confrontation with Maxwell. Now Maxwell asked Joe McGowan, Mackie's successor, to put to the Federated Chapel his request for a mass meeting to be called on the day of the launch, so that the workforce could decide which of the two was to go. Under the constitution of the company only the Federated Chapel or the Executive Council could call a mass meeting.

McGowan and his chapel went into session and passed another motion expressing no confidence in Mackie. McGowan then agreed to call a Federated Chapel meeting which took place in the early hours of Friday, August 15.

Not unexpectedly the Federated Chapel meeting was sparsely attended and several of the prominent FoCs were not present, including the Imperial Father, James Crossan and his deputy Ron Gibson. McGowan took the chair. After a short and ill-tempered debate the Federated Chapel censured both Mackie and Maxwell for speaking out of turn to the Press and ruled that no mass meeting should be held until four weeks after the launch of the tabloid.

While the Federated Chapel were meeting Maxwell was walking into the building after recording an interview in Edinburgh for Radio Forth's 'Forum' programme. During the interview he had revived his obsession with a 24-hour paper. Unless the executive acceded to this plan, he said, he would print his own Glasgow evening newspaper from Albion Street, hiring plant and office space from the co-operative. The wire services were already running the story of Maxwell's latest ploy and it came as a complete surprise to

the Federated Chapel. Maxwell was asked in to the meeting
to explain his statement. He confirmed that if the Executive
Council did not start an evening paper 'promptly' he and a
consortium of friends would be ready to do it. If it was a
success, he added, it would be offered to the co-operative.

Maxwell's latest attempt to force the removal of Mackie
had failed because of the vote at the Federated Chapel. But
it was becoming obvious that the rearguard action being
fought by the compositor to salvage his dream of industrial
harmony would fail at the acid test — a mass meeting —
which had to come sooner or later. His support in the
workforce had all but disintegrated before the cyclonic gusto
of Robert Maxwell. It was not what the man said or did, it
was what he was: successful, ruthless, three times a
millionaire by his own reckoning, who had it within his
resources to staunch the financial haemorrhage from the
project. What had Allister Mackie to offer except a vision,
dogged resilience and an entrée into the lower ranks of the
Labour Party? Robert Maxwell could, and did, phone up top
businessmen, industrialists and politicians. And he could,
and did, drag trade union leaders out of conference to speak
to him on the phone when local union officials had been
trying unsuccessfully for weeks to contact their bosses.
Maxwell might not be too concerned with the niceties of
human relations but he knew the points of leverage in the
City, how to give and extract favours and patronage.
Ordinary people, workers like Allister Mackie, could charge
themselves senseless against entrenched success, Maxwell
only had to pick up the telephone.

Allister Mackie could feel the ground shifting beneath
him:

'It is one of the sad features that when groups of
people, whether workers on the *Daily News* or
elsewhere, find a problem arising within a democratic
set-up there is this terrible built-in tendency to replace
the democratic set-up with an autocratic one. But, you
know, at the end of the day the problem is still there
and it still must be resolved. And you really do not hide
problems by passing it from your own shoulders on to
another individual's shoulders. Any problem that we
have in our company can only be resolved by the co-
operative and by the spirit of co-operation and nothing

129

must be sacrificed in the interest of the temporary problem.'

The problem, of course, was the continuing cash drain. The tabloid circulation began to fall away in the second week, just at the time when it should, on Maxwell's reckoning, have risen on the strength of the difference in price between the *Daily News* and the *Daily Record.* Advertising too, while it had risen slightly, was at nothing like the level needed to sustain the newspaper at the lower price. These two areas, circulation and advertising, were the specific responsibility of Robert Maxwell. Yet he was still able to deflect any criticism away from himself. The weekly losses were now running at £17,000 a week, an improvement, certainly, on the broadsheet days, but an insupportable drain on the precious reserves. Maxwell defended himself, characteristically, by saying that he could only *really* begin to save the situation when he had full executive powers. Allister Mackie and his supporter on the Works Council, James Russell, as well as the leading professional managers, all described the decision to lower the price as 'suicidal' and pointed out that, with the additional revenue brought in by the higher cover price the newspaper would be close to breaking even. Maxwell argued that the only reason the *Daily News* was selling the number of papers it now was — about 170,000 copies — was because of the 1p difference in price. It was a bitter, continuing, spiralling argument.

Robert Maxwell, however, had a new strategy to end the merry-go-round of accusations, which he hoped would force his opponents, like Mackie and Russell, from the executive. This would have the effect of leaving him to exercise his role as chief executive without opposition. He began to accuse the two men in public and over the Tannoy system, of seeking to destroy the *Scottish Daily News,* and plotting to throw 500 men and women on the streets. It was an extraordinary accusation, even by Maxwell's standards, and even the most ardent Maxwell supporter thought he had over-played his hand as he began, shortly after six o'clock on September 3, to make a Tannoy announcement to the workforce:

'Attention. This is Robert Maxwell speaking. We have doubled our circulation. What a time to pick by these terrible people, the enemy in our midst, to destroy our courage and our reputation. I want you to reflect carefully on what I have said. Now is the time when you have got to stand up and make up your mind — either you want the management and leadership I have provided, or else you can take the situation which Mackie and Russell and their ilk have brought about.

'The DTI has asked me to go to a meeting on Tuesday. I cannot go to that meeting with a divided voice. I think that you ought to know that Mr Mackie, without notice to me, has taken a decision to increase the price of our newspaper to 6p from September 21. This increase would be suicidal to our credit and our livelihood.

'I held up a cheque of Beaverbrook for £59,000 because they have not yet fulfilled their promises on machinery. In addition Beaverbrook owe this company £40,000. Mackie insists that it be sent and signed the cheque without my permission.

'I am sorry to give you this dreadful news. This is Mackie and Russell, for reasons of their own, who wish to play politics with the safety of your job. Now is the time to let your feelings be known.

'I have ordered (*sic*) the caseroom management to tell Allister Mackie that he should do a full day's work for the money he gets. It is therefore up to you. I want to hear from your chapel representatives what you want to do to save your jobs. Thank you and goodnight.'

Eleven days later Maxwell made a more specific attack on his enemies. He accused Mackie and Russell of seeking to put the company into liquidation. His voice was strident and highly emotional, and he demanded the rooting out of those he called 'the enemy within . . . those people who are playing politics with your jobs.'

Scottish News Enterprises Limited was now tottering on the brink of insolvency, as a financial report prepared by company secretary William Wolfe showed. It was the presentation of this report to the Department of Industry which formed the basis for Maxwell's accusations. It was, he claimed, a document recommending the liquidation of the company. This must not be allowed to happen, he said, and demanded that a mass meeting be held so that the workforce could show their feelings about 'these terrible people'. The meeting, he ended, must take place the following day, Monday, September 15, at twelve noon. The acid test had come.

Just over 300 members of the workforce attended the meeting on the editorial floor in Albion Street; others boycotted it because it was, strictly speaking, unconstitutional. Maxwell had prepared a statement to the workforce and each person was given a copy under strict orders that it be kept secret.

The first item on the four-point agenda called for a motion approving the holding of the meeting. It was passed overwhelmingly. The second item was the election of a chairman, and the third called for a vote of no confidence in Mackie and the resignation of the company's directors en bloc, although allowing them to seek re-election.

The final item was 'R. Maxwell's proposals for additional capital injection by himself and others in order that an application can be made to the Government to provide further capital of up to £250,000 to enable us to have an additional reserve in case advertising and circulation revenues do not live up to projections in 1976.'

It had been widely predicted that Maxwell was on the point of investing a large sum of money in the company. His opponents saw this as the final strategy to take over the company; his supporters saw it as his attempt to save their jobs. The agenda made no mention of how much Maxwell was prepared to put up, nor did the secret memo which he had distributed earlier. But the general feeling was that it would be — had to be — several hundred thousand pounds. However this would not be known until after the result of Maxwell's demands for the removal of Mackie and Russell was decided by the meeting. The last part of the package was irresistible, but the workforce had to buy the rest of the package first before they knew what was in it.

Maxwell's confidential memo to the workforce opened with his usual comradely address:

Dear Fellow Co-operators,

1. On July 30 last, some seven weeks ago, at the request of the majority of the workforce, I was recalled and given executive powers to try and make a success of the relaunch into tabloid and to increase our

advertising revenue so as to make the paper viable in the shortest possible time.

2. As is well known our circulation for the last week of the broadsheet was approximately 80,000, our current circulation is approximately 170,000 to 180,000, so it can truly be said that we have more than doubled our circulation.

3. Our advertising revenue is equally more than doubled and our intake of advertisements from national and local advertisers as well as the Government is on the increase.

4. Because of 2 and 3 above, our losses, which were running in the early part of August well in excess of £30,000 will reduce this week to approximately £17,000. Our projections for increases in advertising revenue and income from other sources lead me to project our losses for the last quarter of this year will be reduced to average between £10,000 and £12,500 per week and during the first quarter of 1976 I am confident that we will be at break-even point.

5. We have a substantial six-figure cash balance and are paying our bills as they fall due. Our company is fully solvent.

The attempts by Mr Wolfe, Mr Mackie, Mr Russell, Mr McNamara and some others to push this company into liquidation is as unnecessary as it is despicable. If these irresponsible elements are allowed to continue to hold any position of authority in this company then it can only result in one thing — the closure of the paper and loss of your jobs. I am sure that 99% of you want no such thing and will take the necessary steps at this meeting to stop it and to make it clear that you will no longer tolerate anyone in our midst playing 'politics' or irresponsible games with the security of our paper and its 500 jobs.

6. No newspaper in the present economic climate can expect to be profitable within its first year.

In spite of all the hard work by you the workforce since last May in getting the paper out, the company has lost a great deal of money, a lot more than it should have done had it been effectively managed. Equally had it had a proper strategy and effective support to get advertising, the volume of advertising would not have been as abysmally low as it was. The responsibility for this disaster belongs to the Executive Council and not to the hard-working advertising sales force. These matters, as you know, are being put right successfully and will improve substantially over the next two to six months.

7. At today's mass meeting you must decide whether you are going to clear those people out who are in favour of liquidating and give your authority to me and those members of the Executive Council who are for continuing the paper in business and for doing their utmost to make a success of it. The following members of the Executive Council are against liquidation: Mr A. Blyth, Mr N. Goldberg, Mr R. Maxwell, Mr F. Sillitto.

If that is your decision I assure you we will have no difficulty in preventing this calamity.

Finally, because of Mr Wolfe's alarmist statement together with Mr Mackie and Mr Russell's support of it, it is clear that the company will need a cash injection of the order of £200,000, not because we require it now but as an assurance that if our projections on advertising and sales do not materialise within the next six months we shall have a reserve to fall back on to see us through. This is normal business practice. I am prepared to make a contribution of additional capital and know that others are also prepared to do so. Many members of the workforce have intimated to me that they themselves would be prepared to make some additional investment as a way of securing that the paper is given a fair chance of success.

I am sure that once we have ended the internal squabbles and got Mr Mackie and his friends off the Executive Council and back to doing a job of work for which they are paid to do (*sic*) all will be well. Finally, I am optimistic that we shall have no difficulty in getting support from the Government and other sources to enable us to get the additional financial reserves should it be required.

Allister Mackie, still the company chairman, did not hear about the mass meeting until shortly before it started and he had no intention of participating in what he judged to be an unconstitutional gathering. He drove in from his home in Bathgate and arrived in the building as the third item on the agenda — his removal from office — was being bitterly debated. Walking on to the editorial floor he was booed by some of the workforce. He made a short statement, saying that if the workforce went along with Maxwell they would be 'losing their morality'. Denny Macgee, in his best mock-Socratic style, asked whether a document recommending liquidation had been presented to the DTI at the Saturday meeting.

Liquidation had been an option in the conclusion to the financial statement, Mackie replied, but it had been the third option. Two others preceded it: because of the cash crisis the *Daily News* was in, upwards of £250,000 would have to be found, either from an additional loan from the Government or, if the Government would relax the security it held on the building, by raising the money on the commercial market against the value of the property.

Mackie's quiet words of explanation were lost in an angry babble and he left the meeting shortly before he and Jim Russell and William Wolfe lost their seats on the Executive Council by an estimated 300 votes to twelve.

A little later Mackie showed his disillusion at a press conference: 'Following the decision of the workforce today, who decided to give total support to Robert Maxwell's strategy in running the paper, and more or less burying the concept of the co-operative, I view that this is acting against the interests of the co-operative principles that I have always believed in, and on account of this I decided to resign.

'I don't blame the workforce. They have a problem. But they won't resolve their problem by doing this. Because the problems must be faced and as far as I am concerned any problems that arise within a co-operative can only be resolved by applying co-operative principles.'

William Wolfe, the Scottish National Party chairman, was not at the mass meeting to hear himself accused by Robert Maxwell of attempting to liquidate the company to benefit newspaper proprietor — and fellow Nationalist — Sir Hugh Fraser. Wolfe, an accountant, had been company secretary for only ten days. 'I was not present at the meeting. I didn't know about the meeting being held by the workforce. All I have done as company secretary is to make a report to the chairman and to the board as to the position as I saw it. It is a legal responsibility which the company secretary has and I have carried it out.'

Did he suggest in his report that the company should go into liquidation? 'No. I pointed out that the company was in a rather serious position and Mr Maxwell himself has admitted in the statements which he's made that cash is needed. And I pointed out that the alternative — and Mr Maxwell must realise this, and the workforce — that the alternative to getting more money is to go into liquidation.'

Sources of that additional money was the final item on the agenda. Now that Maxwell had destroyed his opposition within the company, the way was clear for him to take total control. In order to have a newspaper to control he would have to provide, from some source, a substantial amount of money. As he stood up to detail what he, personally, was prepared to invest, there was a ripple of relieved optimism, that Maxwell was now going to banish for ever the insecurity and fear by putting in a much larger cheque than his first £100,000. The mood changed markedly when he made it clear in his first few sentences that his investment was to be only £25,000, less than enough to cover two weeks' losses, and that even that was dependent on the workforce investing £50,000 out of their own wages. Most of Maxwell's entrenched opponents had already left the meeting, but nevertheless there was a chatter of disgruntlement as the men realised, perhaps for the first time, that unqualified support for Robert Maxwell did not after all, ensure job security.

The National Union of Journalists' chapel committee met shortly afterwards to discuss what they saw clearly as a disturbing and fundamentally anti-trade union element in the package — the workers had to give up part of their wages and a means-test committee was to be set up to enquire into the finances of those who did not subscribe. The committee decided, unanimously, that NUJ members would not be called before any such committee and would resist any attempt to coerce its members. This decision was communicated to the new chairman of the Executive Council, Alister Blyth. Despite this protest, however, Blyth issued a memo the next day, addressed to all members of staff, which included the sentence: 'Those who feel they

136

cannot contribute on hardship or other grounds, will be given the opportunity to discuss their case with a special committee selected from the Federated Chapel and Works Council.' NUJ officials refused to distribute the memo to journalists until this sentence was struck out and the committee idea scrapped, which happened a day or two later.

Robert Maxwell, now the unchallenged boss, held a press conference immediately after the mass meeting at which, looking tired and emotional, he faced some awkward questions from reporters:

Q. Do you think that Mr Mackie, Mr Wolfe and some others were trying to put the company into liquidation?

Maxwell: Whether you're right or not is a matter for you to judge.

Q. I've seen a document from you alleging that.

Maxwell: If you've seen a document you'll have to produce it.

Q. I'll do that if you want . . .

Maxwell: Then do it.

Q. (producing document) May I quote from it?

Maxwell: It's a confidential document. You may not quote from it.

Q. Well, are you denying that you said that?

Maxwell: No, I'm telling you that it is a confidential document and you are playing with the safety of 500 jobs. And I'm saying that's irresponsible journalism on your part.

Q. Mr Maxwell, is it true or is it not that you've accused Mr Mackie of trying to put the company into liquidation?

Maxwell: That is a matter which I am not prepared to discuss with you.

Q. I understand that the mass meeting was told today that you're somewhere in the region of £250,000 short and that that is required to keep things going?

Maxwell: The answer to your question is that we are very solvent, we have no financial problems.

Q. Why then are you asking workers to take a cut in their wages?

Maxwell: We're asking nobody to take a cut in their wages.

Q. Why then are you asking workers to donate a half of their wages once per month?

Maxwell: We're not asking them to donate half their wages once per month.

Q. Sorry, have they volunteered then?

Maxwell: Certainly.

Q. Who made the request?

Maxwell: If I may say so you can either conduct this conversation in some kind of civilised manner otherwise I shall leave you to it.

Q. I thought I was being perfectly civilised.

Maxwell: You're not being perfectly civilised. I have given you a statement as Chief Executive of this company that this company is solvent. You went on with some cock and bull statements about cutting wages. You've no right to do that. What authority do you claim?

Q. I was merely asking, Mr Maxwell . . .

Maxwell (thumping table): You weren't asking, you were telling, which is something quite bloody different. When that is denied as not being true you then come up with some other thing. I mean, what is it? Are you interested in something else? If it's something else well then go home. As a journalist, and we're in the media, I'm perfectly willing to answer questions.

Q. Is the *Daily News* short of money, Mr Maxwell?

Maxwell: No, I've repeated . . . what is the use of talking to you guys, I mean clearly we ought to forget it. I told you half an hour ago that if every business in the United Kingdom was as well off for cash and paid its bills as promptly as this company there would be no crisis. Have you got cotton wool in your ears?

Q. No, I have not sir.

Maxwell: Well what is it, why are you coming back with this rubbishy question?

Q. I find it strange asking investors for money at a later stage if you don't think, now, that at a later stage you might be short of money. That seems quite common logic to me.

Maxwell: Well if that seems common logic to you that shows why you are never going to run a business.

Q. Is it true, Mr Maxwell, that the company is losing £17,000 a week.

Maxwell: It is losing money. We do not know how accurately. And if you can give it that kind of precision I can't. All newspapers have a running-in period like all new businesses.

Q. I'm quoting your own figures, Mr Maxwell.

Maxwell: I've said that is a confidential document which I'm not prepared to discuss.

Robert Maxwell had finally won the battle which started on March 28, 1974, when he imposed last-minute conditions on his investment. But the peace that was to follow was short-lived, and the *Daily News* was once again to be riven by factional disputes over the rotund publishing entrepreneur from Oxford, by way of Czechoslovakia, who claimed Scotland as his adopted home.

10
Death Throes

In the days after the removal of Mackie and Russell from the Executive Council (to be replaced by two Maxwell supporters, Dorothy-Grace Elder and Tommy Clarke), Maxwell's pervasive influence was felt in every department of the building, but particularly in the caseroom and the editorial where the heartland of his support lay. Yet despite an acutely sensitive political nose, the man was capable of gross errors of miscalculation. In the first week he made two which provoked an angry backlash among journalists. The first, on the Thursday of the week he took control, centred on a memo he sent to the editor and senior editorial staff. It set out to detail the measures Maxwell felt necessary to preserve and improve the newspaper, but it was done in such a grossly intrusive fashion that, had it happened in the Beaverbrook regime, it would have caused a production stoppage and bitter controversy.

The content of the paper, Maxwell said, was dull and overly serious. The first paragraph of his statement of ideas was hardly a model for a new and vigorous writing style.

Now that the squabbles in our Boardroom are over and the workforce has expressed its overwhelming desire that it wishes to continue to work for a commercially successful paper and have confirmed their vote by agreeing to put their hands in their pockets to put up additional investment in the paper, it is incumbent upon those of us who have a major responsibility in the management and content of the *Scottish Daily News* to give urgent and careful consideration as to what steps must be taken in order to produce a newspaper which will be bought by more and more people and in sufficient quantity to attract advertisers in exactly the same way as our successful rivals do.

The first priority as far as I am concerned, is therefore the identification of the target audience to whom our newspaper intends to serve, and to create a paper and adopt a formula that will appeal to our audience. We must agree that we cannot be all things to all men.

The paper must be consistent in personality, something that has not happened since its launch.

The paper is probably too serious at present, both in content and presentation. Subbing is dull and quite often spoils good content.

We lack name writers, a matter which must be remedied.

We must develop a great deal more reader participation: competitions etc.

We must adopt a national posture which is easily recognised by our readers.

The editor and the senior editorial staff and all members of the editorial staff must be conscious at all times over the next few months that they should go for stories which can help advertising and circulation whenever they possibly can.

We desperately lack advertising on the retailing side and I and Jimmy Galt will be concentrating on this aspect immediately, with the target of getting in as advertisers, some twenty retailers.

Maxwell also contributed a column to the paper, the first of what was to be an occasional series. His article did little to bolster the flagging features pages, being typically egocentric and tortuously constructed. It dealt with his peasant heritage and his identification with, and adoption of, Scotland — a link which did nothing to endear him to the Nationalists on the staff. However, it was the abuse of the NUJ rule book — in which chapels are instructed not to accept non-union contributions on a regular basis from those other than specialists in a particular field — which called up the second storm.

As a result of complaints from several journalists about the incursion into the domain of the NUJ by Maxwell, a chapel committee meeting was called. Two journalists had already referred the incident to the Glasgow branch of the union since they had no confidence that the FoC, George Welsh — who had voted for Maxwell's package of proposals on the Monday — could impartially interpret the rule book. The branch chairman's response had been that there were so many non-union writers contributing regularly — and indeed there were several journalists working in Albion Street who did not belong to the NUJ — that action could not be taken solely on the Maxwell article. Fortunately the *SDN* chapel committee decided to instruct the editor not to print any further Maxwell contributions, thereby avoiding a messy confrontation.

The financial situation of the company was by this time critical, and deteriorating. Maxwell had admitted to the workforce, if not the outside world, that an injection of at least £250,000 was necessary to take the newspaper through the winter. He had agreed to put in up to £25,000 and around half the workforce had pledged one and a half weeks salary over three months, or around £20,000. On Friday, September 19, the financial imbalance took a lurch for the worse when Beaverbrook took legal action to seize from the *Daily News* funds over £59,000 they claimed was still owed on the sale of the building to the co-operative. This move by Beaverbrook had been anticipated even before the relaunch of the tabloid and Maxwell had, in fact, removed what remained of the *Daily News* bank balance from the Bank of Scotland.

But what the Beaverbrook litigation did finally was to destroy any vestiges of financial credibility that still remained — particularly as the *SDN* led on Saturday with a splash headline, 'Beaverbrook Raid on *News* Cash', with a sub-head, 'It's a Bloody Disgrace'. Overnight, credit facilities dried up, bills had to be paid on the spot and the accounts department was swamped with invoices from creditors scenting extinction. Reporters no longer had credit lines for taxis, petrol for the two editorial cars had to be bought with cash and re-claimed and photographic supplies were only to be obtained cash on the nail.

Ironically, one of the last executive actions of Allister Mackie and Jimmy Russell had been to write a cheque for the money to Beaverbrook, which was owing as VAT

142

charges. This had been countermanded by Maxwell after the two were deposed and before the cheque could be sent out. There was no disagreement that the company owed Beaverbrook the money but Robert Maxwell maintained that he had made a private arrangement with Jocelyn Stevens over newsprint which meant, he claimed, that the co-operative was owed some £30,000. There was no written documentation, but Maxwell insisted that the deal stood and would not allow the VAT cheque to be paid. Beaverbrook, however, were denying that any agreement existed and they took legal action to seize the *Daily News* funds which, although it was unsuccessful in recovering the money owed, effectively destroyed the company's financial credibility.

The next day, Sunday, saw the final blow to the staggering company, an investigative article in the *Sunday Times* (now the subject of litigation) titled 'How Maxwell Sabotaged the Workers' Dream'. The article traced the irresistible business rise of Robert Maxwell and his takeover of the *Scottish Daily News*. Perhaps understandably in a workforce numbed by accusations and factional infighting, the article provoked little response; those who wanted to believe it did, those who didn't put it down to a vendetta by the newspaper and the Establishment against a foreign-born maverick. Dazed and increasingly unenthusiastic, the 500 workers got on with doing their jobs, which all but the most optimistic now saw would be short-lived.

In the week before the publication of the *Sunday Times* article, the three reporters responsible, Ian Jack, Phillip Knightley and James Fox, had been in Glasgow interviewing staff on both sides of the Maxwell division. Ian Jack, a former chief sub-editor on the *Scottish Daily Express,* knew many of the journalists in Albion Street and, indeed, had been tentatively approached by the co-operative in the early days to be editor of the new newspaper. But it was a man whose by-line did not appear on the article, Insight editor Bruce Page, whom Maxwell saw as the orchestrator of a defamatory campaign against him and Page was cited as a defendant in Maxwell's libel actions on the story.

On the following Saturday the *Daily News* called a press conference in London to rebut the charges made in the article. In the early hours of Saturday morning Robert Maxwell phoned the *Daily News* copy takers to dictate an addition to a detailed rebuttal telex which had been sent hours before to the *Sunday Times*. The addition, a paragraph in length, was approved by deputy editor Nathan Goldberg in the absence of Fred Sillitto who was in England attending his daughter's wedding. Around two in the morning, a nightshift reporter checking the wire machines for late news came across the telex and the added paragraph, in which Maxwell described the *Sunday Times* report as the 'shittiest and most disgraceful piece of journalism in the history of British newspapers'. The reporter, cringing at the addition, called night editor Jack Wills into the room — Nathan Goldberg had left — and Wills immediately intimated to FoC George Welsh that if that paragraph appeared in the *Sunday Times* he would resign, and he suggested to Welsh that he should use his powers to kill the paragraph and censure Maxwell.

Shortly before the press conference was due to start Welsh, unable to contact Goldberg and company chairman Alister Blyth, phoned Denny Macgee the other deputy editor, relayed the earlier happenings and intimated the disgust of the journalists who had read the telex. Macgee phoned the London hotel where the press conference was due to take place and spoke to Maxwell, telling him that in the interests of the *Daily News* he, Maxwell, should ensure that the paragraph was struck out of the telex. Macgee reminded Maxwell that if *Sunday Times* editor Harold Evans decided to print the telex in full the *Daily News* would not only be the laughing stock of the press, but it would be resorting to exactly the 'gutter type of journalism which we were complaining about in the first instance'.

In a typewritten statement to the NUJ chapel committee about the incident Macgee said:

'I was alarmed that Mr Maxwell should take it upon himself to word a paragraph in this manner without consultation with the editor under whose name the article was appearing. I decided to contact the editor who was weekending in England to attend his daughter's wedding. He was shocked to hear the wording of the message. He said that an attempt had been made at an earlier stage of the compilation of the article to use the word "shittiest" but that he had deleted it from the text. He said he would resign immediately if the paragraph appeared under his name in this manner. He further instructed me to take every possible step to make certain anything likely to act against the good name of the *Scottish Daily News* in the paragraph be excluded.

'To comply with this request I tried to contact Alister Blyth at the London hotel where the press conference was being held. He was addressing the meeting but would be finished in two minutes if I cared to hold on. A little later Mr Maxwell came to the phone and insultingly told me not to behave like a child.

'I consider this gross impudence, especially coming from the man who in the first instance was guilty of a serious indiscretion in the wording of the communication to one editor purporting to come from the editor of the *Scottish Daily News*.

'The really important aspect of this whole matter is, however, the increasing trend by Mr Maxwell to influence the editorial content of this newspaper and in this instance to assume he has the authority to speak on its behalf.'

In any event the *Sunday Times* edited the last paragraph and Wills and Sillitto were not forced to resign. A resignation did come, however, from the most unexpected of sources. On Friday, October 3, five days after the *Sunday Times* published a precis of the massive telex from the *Scottish Daily News* in their letters column — without retracting the allegations in their article about the manner in which Robert Maxwell had taken over stewardship of the paper — the man at the centre of the dispute walked away. For his own reasons Robert Maxwell walked out of Albion Street. A mass meeting urged him, by 248 votes to eighteen, to stay with the company 'to prove to the world in due time that we are not just a social experiment, not a motley assortment of 500 industrial guinea-pigs, but that we are a responsible and dedicated workforce whose enterprise is the shape of the future.'

Maxwell charged the *Sunday Times* with 'character assassination', which had put the future of the newspaper in jeopardy. As he left, no one in the building, supporters or opponents, believed that he was abandoning the enterprise, but rather that he was keeping out of the way in Oxford, still pulling the strings, allowing the furore to dissipate before being popularly recalled, once again, to save the situation. Robert Maxwell must have known by then that the situation had become irredeemable.

'I would have liked to have acceded [to the request to stay on]' [he said before catching the London plane] 'but given these malicious attacks by the *Sunday Times* and others inspired, at least some of it by the people inside such as Mr Mackie and Mr Russell and a few others, I really had to remove myself from the battle in order to give the newspaper a chance to carry on its business in calm waters, in a professional way, as it is doing.'

Did he feel bitter?

'I certainly felt very upset by the way I've been attacked, in particular about being called a Fascist [the *Sunday Times* article included an alleged confrontation between Mackie and Maxwell in which the deposed chairman told Maxwell that he should destroy his Labour Party card and join the National Front because he was a Fascist at heart, at which, allegedly, Maxwell smiled].

'I fought against Hitler, was wounded several times — I mean like millions of other people. I did my bit during the war. But to couple this, the bulk of my family were annihilated by the Nazis and the last thing you can throw at a person like myself is the epithet of being a Fascist.'

A week earlier Professor Richard Briston, the financial adviser, had resigned:

'The basic reason was that the firm of accountants in which I'm a partner (French and Cowan) had been asked to resign as auditors and another firm of accountants (Coopers Lybrand, Pergamon's accountants) had been asked to take over and I felt it was rather an invidious position to be in. So although I was asked to remain as a financial adviser I thought it better from a professional point of view to resign.

'It was all decided at an Executive Council meeting to which I was not invited and I only heard about it when my firm received the letter asking them to resign.

Initially my reaction was one of surprise because after I'd been asked expressly not to attend the meeting I found that an item like that was being discussed, which was rather underhand.'

Maxwell had claimed that his return to the management of the newspaper had saved it from disaster. Briston, however, disagrees.

'Certainly the paper was not flourishing at the time he came back but the direct result of his intervention at that stage was the withdrawal of the general manager, the chief accountant, the reduction of the paper from 6p to 5p, all of which I think had a disastrous effect. The important decision which I think did help the paper considerably, namely to go tabloid, had already been made before he returned, was already under way under the supervision of the general manager.

'It's quite clear that he hadn't saved the situation because there was already talk that more finance was needed. In the second place, there was no evidence at all that the situation was better than it would have been had he not intervened. My own opinion is, if anything, that it was worse.'

Briston, who had been introduced into the co-operative by Maxwell, watched with growing alarm the manner of the man's accretion of power:

'His style of managerial behaviour has already been analysed in depth in a series of Government reports and I wouldn't want to attract a writ by referring to those. But I feel that there is a great deal of truth in the things that are said about his managerial style. The way he behaved at Executive Council meetings where, if, for example, a vote went against him he would say on occasion well. I don't care how you vote, I'm going to do things my way. Or even if he didn't say that, he would take steps which would commit the paper to the course of action which he wanted.'

There was now little time left to the co-operative, creditors were growing increasingly persistent and it was becoming difficult even to obtain newsprint. The 24-hour newspaper idea had been resuscitated in an attempt to tap additional pools of advertising and circulation. The factor to be overcome in the liquidity calculation on the 24-hour paper — in essence the *Daily News* with a supplementary evening edition for the Strathclyde region — was the increased cost of salaries, newsprint, distribution. But by lobbying the plan with the Government, persuading them that here was the vital lifeline, the paper's management hoped to winnow out further finance, either in cash or through a relaxation of the security the Government held on Albion Street, to enable the company to survive into the New Year. There was, however, a new ethos in the Industry Ministry and the Cabinet: support to lame ducks had ended with the removal of Tony Benn and the Government were sticking firmly to the letter of their loan terms with the co-operative. There would be no further finance.

In the dog days following the departure of Maxwell the content of the newspaper became more and more self-obsessed, issuing a daily catalogue of its rebuffs, appealing to the 'people of Scotland' to support the fight to retain 500 jobs. A new editor had been appointed, Nathan Goldberg, a Communist who, nevertheless, had been one of Maxwell's strongest supporters throughout. Goldberg took over from Fred Sillitto on the heels of Maxwell's abandonment of Albion Street. Sillitto moved into an ill-defined job, ostensibly in charge of the paper's leader columns.

Any impetus or dynamism that a new editor could provide was, by this stage, irrelevant — the paper was doomed. Goldberg, when asked how he felt about taking over an editor compared himself to the captain of the Titanic. From then on he was known as Nathan Iceberg.

Meetings with the Department of Trade and Industry and Bruce Millan, Minister of State at the Scottish Office, were now taking place several times a week, with the Government stonewalling every plea for additional funding. The *News* line was that if the Government would ease back their secured creditor status the co-operative could raise capital using the building and plant as security. But the Government continued to insist that Albion Street was their security on the loan and that could not be relaxed: there was a duty to the taxpayer to safeguard the investment.

On Monday, October 6, the day Nathan Goldberg officially took over as editor, a letter arrived at Albion Street from Bruce Millan rejecting the company's cash approaches and confirming that the conditions on the £1.2m loan — that it would be a once-and-for-all injection — would remain. This stimulated a bitter editorial outburst from Goldberg against the Government, calling their decision 'beyond belief'.

Most of the workers still believed, probably because reality was too horrendous to contemplate, that there would be an eleventh-hour reprieve, either in the form of a climb-down by the Government in the face of 500 redundancies, or in the form of an offer for the paper from Maxwell.

On Friday, October 17, company chairman Alister Blyth came over the Tannoy to tell the workforce that there was to be a crucial mass meeting on the editorial floor on Monday, at which important information concerning their futures would be put to the workers. The building was abuzz with rumour and conjecture over the weekend as different scenarios were propounded and compounded. The commonly expressed view was that the Government, faced with the political embarrassment of the 500 survivors of the Beaverbrook withdrawal about to join the dole queues again, would allow the paper to raise finance by relaxing the loan condition. Some saw this as a scene-setter for a triumphal re-emergence of Robert Maxwell from his self-imposed exile.

When the meeting opened, however, Alister Blyth unveiled a totally unforeseen manoeuvre, the appointment of a provisional liquidator to take over the running of the paper. Most of those gathered understood the implications of liquidation, but not this concept of 'provisional liquidation'. Blyth explained that provisional liquidation would protect the company from being wound up by outside creditors, which seemed likely and imminent, and the liquidation was redeemable if the man appointed to manage it — Blyth asked the workforce to accept Mr James Whitton of the accountants Coopers Lybrand — was able to raise enough capital to allow the company to meet its bills and trade profitably.

Blyth stressed that Whitton's paramount task was to preserve the newspaper, the main asset in liquidation, and through it the 500 jobs involved. He could sell the paper as a going concern to anyone who wanted it, appeal for fresh investment or finally, if all else failed, he would split up the assets and sell for what he could get. But, Blyth underlined, the company's strongest asset was the *Daily News,* selling 150,000 a day, and the workforce should strive to consolidate, or improve that circulation, thereby increasing the attractiveness of their asset and their own chances of continued working. This measure, he said, was the only one the company could take due to the hostile financial tides washing round Albion Street. The appointment of a provisional liquidator, sanctioned by the court, would enable the company's credit to be guaranteed and wages to be paid, until such time as Whitton decided that all possible avenues had been explored and the winding-up of the company was the only course left.

After the meeting had agreed to Whitton's appointment Alister Blyth met the Press:

'The Executive Council of the *Scottish Daily News* passed the unanimous resolution this morning, subsequently ratified by the unanimous decision from the workforce. The resolution reads — "Due to the financial position of the company the Executive Council of the *Scottish Daily News* resolved that in the interests of its workers and creditors and to ensure continuation of the *Scottish Daily News,* to instruct its solicitors to petition the court for the appointment of Mr James Whitton as provisional liquidator. Meanwhile vigorous attempts will be made to persuade the Government to facilitate the raising of fresh capital. The possibility of finding a purchaser for the building will also be fully explored. The immediate financial problem faced by the *Scottish Daily News* arises in the main from its inability to raise further finance following the *Sunday Times* recent attack on the *Scottish Daily News*." '

Two days later the court approved the appointment of Whitton and the provisional liquidator took over the running of the company from the Executive Council. The workers' co-operative was now officially dead. On Tuesday members of the powerless Executive Council met Harold Wilson at Downing Street, still lobbying for a relaxation in the loan conditions. With 500 more about to join the 30,000 dole queue in Glasgow they were intent on impressing on the Prime Minister that the £250,000 the company was seeking should be measured against the unemployment and social security benefits that would result, and the loss of political capital to the Government in Scotland where its balance of power was gravely threatened by the SNP. The meeting with the Prime Minister, and the arguments advanced, produced no thaw in the Cabinet's attitude.

On October 31 the provisional liquidator told the workforce at a mass meeting that the Government had agreed to a week's stay of execution. Afterwards Alister Blyth announced to the Press that there would be a 'Save the *News*' rally the following day at Custom House Quay, Glasgow. 'While there's life there's hope,' Blyth said, 'and we spent fourteen months in struggle to create this newspaper and people who do that don't give up easily.' On the question of whether Robert Maxwell was interested in buying the building and plant Blyth would not be drawn.

The next day, Saturday, a few hundred people, principally *Daily News* employees, but with a strong SNP presence, gathered to hear a succession of speakers plead for the survival of the newspaper. The platform party could hardly have contained more disparate characters: Norman Buchan, the Labour MP for West Renfrewshire, Teddy Taylor, the high Tory from Cathcart, Margo MacDonald of the SNP, Jimmy Reid (then) of the Communist Party, Jimmy Milne of the Scottish Trades Union Congress, as well as representatives from the Catholic and Protestant churches.

Alister Blyth spoke of the exhilarating experience of working in the co-operative, the need to preserve employment and the threat to democracy by the diminution of the Press. He gave what he saw as the reasons for the current crisis: 'One of the main reasons is that . . . anyone in the newspaper industry will tell you . . . that it takes at least a year for a newspaper to become established, get on its feet to settle its circulation. It became clear that we were underfinanced from the start. We simply did not have enough money to carry us over the initial loss-making period. This was aggravated, of course, by the fact that we came out with the wrong size of newspaper.' Given six months, he went on, the *Daily News* would be viable. But the Government were refusing to amend the condition of their loan, even faced with the imminent loss of 500 jobs in depressed Clydeside.

Margo MacDonald, vice-chairman of the SNP, took up the issue of the failure of the Government to respond to the

Daily News predicament: 'The Government took a responsibility for this co-operative, not just to a newspaper, but to a co-operative and they must see that responsibility through. . . I will consider that I have been sold out and everybody else has been sold out if the Government sits back and allows any entrepreneur — no matter how benevolent — to walk in here. If this was an experiment then the Government will be choking it off halfway through the experiment without giving it a chance to see where it leads.' And all for the sake of 'amending a bookkeeping entry,' as she called it.

The speech from Jimmy Reid was characteristically emotion-charged and quotable: 'The Reverend Gray, Monsigneur Murphy made some reference to the need for a miracle and Nelson (Gray) was saying that he was a professional believer in miracles. The miracle he was referring to was, of course, the Messiah. Let us be clear, no entrepreneur, no financier will be the Messiah for the *Scottish Daily News*. The workers in the *Scottish Daily News*, the trade unions in Scotland and the Scottish people are the ones who have got to resolve today, without any indecisiveness, that this miracle will be achieved.'

Reid, in his usual flamboyance, drew in references from the Bible and from Mao Tse Tung and called on trade unionists and Scottish workers to 'close ranks behind the *Scottish Daily News*', which he saw as one of the focal points in the fight against unemployment. He called on the crowd to demonstrate support in a tangible way, by giving money to the fighting fund: 'Throw your money up here, none of these formal things of passing a plate around.' And more than £500, in coins, crumpled up pounds and hastily written cheques, arced down on the platform.

It was left to the newest director of Scottish News Enterprises, Dorothy-Grace Elder, to close the rally: 'Ladies and gentlemen, we are not going to be ground into the dirt by anyone, we are not going to be forced out of existence by the forces of the capitalist press. We haven't got much money apart from this for our fighting fund but by God we've got guts and we will never surrender. Never! Our paper will continue to be published, somehow — God willing it will be with your help. And I'm going to ask you now, are you ready now to send a message to this Government and to chant it after me . . . SAVE THE *NEWS* . . . SAVE THE

NEWS . . . SAVE THE *SCOTTISH DAILY NEWS* . . . .'

The Government responded by allowing one week's extension, presumably to bring the co-operative up to six months of operation and the employees into earnings-related benefit with 26 National Insurance stamps on their cards. But on November 6, James Whitton announced to a mass meeting that, reluctantly, he would have to close down the paper two days later.

After speaking for fifteen minutes in a rambling, oblique style, he left the meeting to 'pursue the options which remain,' including a tentative offer from Robert Maxwell. Immediately Whitton left, to sycophantic applause from the workforce, Alister Blyth read out a telex which had just arrived from the wealthy publisher.

From Mr Robert Maxwell
To Mr James Whitton
Provisional Liquidator
Scottish News Enterprises

Copy to:
Bruce Millan, Minister of State, Scottish Office
Alister Blyth, Chairman of Executive Council, SDN
Sir Max Aitken, Chairman Beaverbrook Newspaper Ltd
James Milne, General Secretary STUC
All general secretary's of national unions who have members at the *Scottish Daily News*

I should be grateful if you would read out at today's mass meeting my below given message.

A new evening paper for the Glasgow and Strathclyde region to provide employment for many of the journalists and workforce now employed at the *Scottish Daily News* at Albion Street, Glasgow.

1.   Like you and the vast majority cf the people in Scotland, I am both shocked and saddened at the Government's refusal to make the relatively small sum of additional finance available which would have enabled the *Scottish Daily News* to prove itself in the market place over the next 3-6 months. However, now that we know definitely that no money will be forthcoming from that quarter and since no fairy godfather has

appeared on the scene willing to finance the heavy weekly losses incurred by the newspaper, there is no alternative but for the paper to close. Immediately after its closure I intend to start talks with the provisional liquidator, the Government and Beaverbrook Newspapers, members of the Executive Council or Action Committee and trade union representatives about the possibility of launching speedily a Glasgow and Strathclyde region evening paper to compete with the *Evening Times*. These talks will be about the viability of the project, the manning levels and wage scales and to determine the degree of enthusiasm and support which is likely to be forthcoming from the workforce for the launch of this new evening paper which if successful will eventually lead to the launching of the 24-hour paper concept which should provide further substantial employment opportunities in the Strathclyde region.

2. Both as a creditor and substantial investor in the company I have informed the provisional liquidator of my agreement that the surplus that will arise from the liquidation should be used in the first instance for the refunding of the approximately £200,000 invested by you, the workforce. I am sending this appeal to all creditors, including the Government and Beaverbrook newspapers so that they too should give their consent for this to be done. In this way you will at least have refunded to you your original investment.

3. I have made a cash offer to Mr Jocelyn Stevens to purchase the *Daily Express* interest in the Scottish News Enterprises for a six-figure sum. My offer has not been accepted as the *Daily Express* believes it will get a higher sum from the liquidation of the company and the sale of its assets. I hope that the *Daily Express* board will agree to change its mind so as to enable the evening paper proposal to proceed.

4. The blame for the failure of Scottish News Enterprises Ltd does not rest on the shoulders of the journalists or the workforce. In fact, you have performed miracles of production of which there has been no equal in this country. The real blame must clearly rest with the Executive Council who, contrary to the representations made to the DTI and the declara-

154

tion in the original prospectus, decided last April to run the newspaper without a man of proven commercial ability and took it upon themselves to run the day-to-day affairs of the company without the necessary knowledge and experience. The real lesson for the future of any workers' co-operative is that it is not enough to have a skilled and dedicated workforce to produce a product or service, you must also have a highly capable business management team responsible for ensuring the commercial success of the enterprise.

5. In the present harsh economic climate and the Scottish Daily News Enterprises having lost the £1m it was provided with last April it is not possible to continue the *Scottish Daily News* in its present form. What may be feasible is to launch, fairly quickly, an evening newspaper servicing the Glasgow and Strathclyde region. Since the demise of the *Evening Citizen* a great many readers and advertisers in Glasgow and Strathclyde region have been disappointed with the relatively poor performance and service of the *Evening Times*. A survey which I had carried out some while ago confirms that such a new evening paper could count on a minimum circulation of 150,000 copies. The staffing required for this paper is, of course, less than for a daily. The cost of distribution and advertising are also much reduced and I believe that such a newspaper could be made profitable fairly quickly.

6. The new company to run the evening paper would be a limited liability company owned by one of my family companies (not Pergamon Press). I envisage it to be a worker-participation enterprise incorporating a profit-sharing scheme, with half of the 12-member board of directors being elected by the workforce.

Robert Maxwell
Pergamon Press Ltd

The telex which seemed meticulously constructed to flatter, apportion blame and rekindle hope, was badly received. Those who had hypnotically followed the vision of Maxwell and what he represented — a lucrative security — had found it to be a mirage. Reality was to be the dole again, after thirteen months of struggle to create a newspaper, after six brief months of working at their trades again, of freedom from the weekly degradation of the dole queue. The effort that had been put in, the long hours without overtime, the innovation, the pride in producing a paper that really was theirs, that belonged to them down to the waste-basket, had finally been for nothing. There had never been any rational basis for imagining that it would have a different conclusion. Reason, however, had not created the *Scottish Daily News*. And after a brief half-life it was over.

Allister Mackie, the man who came to embody the spirit of the *Daily News* in the black months when wise men told the struggling co-operative to accept reality (the dole queue) never fully believed that the enterprise would work. 'But that', he said 'is no reason to accept that what you're told is the inevitable. It was worth doing, now wasn't it?'

At a further mass meeting on the eve of the closure of the paper the workers met to pledge themselves to sit in, to continue the fight for self-respect that had begun in March 1974. They produced several emergency editions of the paper, printed by a commercial printer, but there was no longer the will to struggle. Staff began to drift away, finally and belatedly accepting the reality forced on them. Some, of course, stayed in Albion Street because there was nowhere else to go. Two of the worker-directors who were determined to salvage something from the collapse, Dorothy-Grace Elder and Alister Blyth, visited Robert Maxwell, the last evaporating hope of saving at least some of the jobs. They took with them copies of one of the emergency issues and some collecting cans. Robert Maxwell peeled off £100 from his bankroll and stuffed it in a can. Events had come full circle.

11
Final Thoughts

In attempting to sum up the significance of the *Scottish Daily News* it is necessary, first of all, to ask what it was. If it was a serious attempt to set up a new, commercially viable newspaper to compete in the already overcrowded Scottish newspaper market, it failed and was almost certainly doomed to failure. If it was a serious attempt to establish a worker-controlled enterprise which would be a test-bed for an alternative to orthodox management structures and capitalist control of the means of the production, the *Scottish Daily News* failed to provide solutions although it left some useful lessons for any future attempt at a similar venture. But if the whole project was no more than a protracted protest by Beaverbrook employees at the fact and the manner of their forced unemployment it was a resounding, expensive success.

In March 1974, 1,850 men and women were told their jobs no longer existed; by all the accepted rules they ought to have conceded that they were dispensable and that a liquidity crisis in Beaverbrook Newspapers Limited was a sufficient and indisputable reason why they should go home and sign on at the labour exchange. Instead, eighteen months after they had been made redundant, the workers — or at least 500 of them — were still working in Albion Street and their enterprise had created waves which will continue to influence events — not just in the newspaper industry — long after Albion Street is broken up and sold off, never to produce another daily newspaper.

When all is said and done, these 500 people did not do the simple, the sensible thing when they were made redundant and, by doggedly refusing to lie down when all around were telling them their struggle was hopeless, they

157

created a unique institution which, in turn, gave them a
unique experience which, in retrospect, most of them
probably reckon was fair recompense for their effort.
Certainly it is an experience which many of their colleagues
in safe jobs and orthodox newspapers privately envied them.

But if the idea of a worker-controlled newspaper was
born as a protest at enforced redundancies, it undoubtedly
became much more than that as the thirteen-month struggle
developed. And once the tabloid newspaper had settled
down, the 500 workers were producing a highly professional,
readable newspaper with the third-highest circulation of any
daily newspaper in Scotland: at 150,000 sales each day, well
ahead of the *Scotsman* and the *Glasgow Herald,* and of the
Aberdeen *Press and Journal* and the Dundee *Courier.* And
the workers were doing it with about half the labour force
which produced the *Scottish Daily Express.* That, as they
say, can't be altogether bad.

So who was to blame for its failure? The Government,
who gave them enough money to start but not enough to
survive? The workers themselves, who threw away their
chance when they had 330,000 sales? Robert Maxwell, who
may have given them the kiss of death along with his
£100,000? The Scottish public, who didn't give them long
enough to sort out early shortcomings? All of them, in various
ways, contributed much that was positive and something that
was harmful. The whole enterprise had such a remote chance
of picking its way through the minefield confronting a new
worker-controlled newspaper that it could not avoid
triggering off its own destruction.

We have seen, throughout this brief history, many
difficulties which would face any worker-controlled operation
trying to survive in a commercial world. Workers, to
perpetuate a crude distinction, know little of the real world of
business and can easily fall into simple errors at their first
attempts. The Action Committee, for instance, thought that
150,000 signatures of people who said they were willing to buy
the *Scottish Daily News* for three months, was a guarantee
that sales would be well in excess of that figure. They didn't
realise — nor did the pioneers of market research — that
people in the street will almost always say 'Yes' to a question
like 'Would you buy my newspaper/soap powder/baked
beans?' simply because it is very hard to say to someone you

don't know that you don't like what he is proposing to produce.

Worker control necessarily requires a higher degree of democracy and shop-floor involvement than traditional capitalist company organisation; if not, the leading workers have become bosses (in organisation, if not in financial terms). But this makes the isolated worker-controlled enterprise highly vulnerable to demagogues from within or without. And, of course, this vulnerability is heightened if, initially, the project is not successful and if, as in the *Scottish Daily News*, the workforce have little hope of alternative employment if the project fails; it is easy to spread panic, especially by misinterpreting complex information like financial accounts and projections.

Eric Tough, a conservative and uncritical supporter of free enterprise, believes a comprehensive educational programme is an essential prerequisite before workers have any hope of successfully running a business. He is correct in the sense that the worker-directors of the *SDN* did not have time to learn enough about running a business to withstand the barrage of pressures which hit them in the first weeks of the project. He is mistaken if he thinks that educating workers means convincing them that profitability is the only goal, commercial considerations the only criteria. If the ex-Beaverbrook workers had taken account of these lessons they would never have started the *Scottish Daily News*.

It must be said that the *Scottish Daily News*, as a newspaper, had little chance of success. The newspaper industry has been contracting for a decade and there is no reason to suppose it will not go on contracting in the future. And the popular newspaper market has declined more than the 'quality'. In Scotland the *Scottish Daily Express* had declined from a peak of 660,000 in 1968 to 570,000 just before the closure of Albion Street. So the *Scottish Daily News* had to carve its circulation out of the declining *Express* readership with, perhaps, some gains from the *Daily Record*, the *Glasgow Herald* and the *Scotsman*. The *Scottish Daily Express* dropped about 100,000 sales following the move to Manchester so, if the *Daily News* was to reach anything like a viable circulation, it would either have to cut into the readership of an existing newspaper or conjure new readers out of the void.

To add to this problem, the *Scottish Daily News* was also launching itself into what Eric Tough describes as 'the worst recession in advertising for twenty years'. It had proclaimed a left-of-centre philosophy which was hardly likely to endear it to potential advertisers and it had no proven circulation, either in numbers or type, to offer. A high advertising content would have bridged the gap if circulation had failed to match up to expectations. In the event — predictably — both fell short.

All this — and much more — was, of course, known to the Government when they finally agreed to lend the co-operative £1.2m. Three factors probably persuaded them, against their better judgment, to release the loan. The electoral threat posed by the Scottish National Party is a guarantee that any project which will improve the Labour Government's image in Scotland will receive more than usually sympathetic consideration. The co-operative was not only offering to save 500 jobs in the depressed West of Scotland but was making such a noise that the political rewards of giving them what they were asking for made saving *these* jobs more than usually worthwhile. And Tony Benn, Secretary of State for Industry, was at the high point of his campaign to establish himself as the darling of the Labour left and the midwife to a whole new world in British industry — the birth of the workers' co-operative to succeed where capitalism had failed.

It is a matter for astonishment and regret that, having finally agreed to lend the co-operative £1.2m, the Government turned down last-minute requests from the leaders of the project to lend them sufficient extra funds to free themselves from the disruptive influence of Robert Maxwell. The Action Committee had learned, too late, what the DTI had already said publicly about Robert Maxwell — that 'he is not in our opinion a person who can be relied on to exercise proper stewardship of a publicly/quoted company.'

And having so hamstrung the co-operative that they had to accept Maxwell's money with all its conditions, the Government then refused to help the project during the last desperate days in September and October because of Maxwell's association with it.

Certainly, it is not difficult to imagine that the

Department of Trade and Industry was deeply embarrassed to find itself supporting with public money a project in which Robert Maxwell was playing a dominant role; clearly they were unlikely to be anxious to extend the level of their commitment.

As to Robert Maxwell himself, one thing should be said: whatever his motives for becoming involved in the *Scottish Daily News* — and he is on record as having said that he still has ambitions to own and help in the management of a newspaper — he devoted a monumental amount of time and energy to the project in addition to the crucial £114,000 he invested in it. His decision to reduce the price from 6p to 5p may well have hastened the end for the *Scottish Daily News*, but without his cheque on March 28 the enterprise would never have started. If he had ambitions to pick up the pieces and give himself a newspaper 'for peanuts' they were frustrated; if he had ambitions to salvage his battered reputation within the Labour movement, he did himself more harm than good; if he genuinely wanted to help the honest workers he inadvertently did *them* more harm than good.

The workforce achieved a great deal and they were within an ace of confounding all their critics when, on May 5, 1975, they produced a newspaper and within days sold 330,000 copies. For these few days over 330,000 people were saying to themselves, 'let's try this new paper we've heard so much about'; they were changing their newspaper buying habits at least to the extent of buying a second newspaper, even if they continued to buy the *Daily Express,* the *Daily Record* or the *Glasgow Herald.* If enough of these people had been sufficiently impressed by the *Scottish Daily News* they would have continued to buy it, either as a second paper or as a substitute for their previous favourite.

Now, the most enthusiastic supporter of the *Scottish Daily News* could not have expected the paper to hold on to that kind of inflated readership. Some people were buying it just to have a copy of one of the first editions; others just wanted to be able to show their friends that they had tried it; others were bound to be put off by something in the paper. But even the sternest critic of the paper must have been surprised at the slump that followed. By the end of the first week the paper was dropping 20,000 readers a day and, if the rate of decline slowed, the decline itself did not stop until September, by which time the damage had been done and only a miracle could have saved the *Scottish Daily News*.

The shortcomings of the contents of the newspaper have been discussed at length elsewhere. The editorial department was not only seriously understaffed but consisted largely, though not entirely, of those former Beaverbrook journalists who had been unable to find a job elsewhere. If the first issues of the *Daily News* had been some of the later tabloid issues the story might have had a very different ending. But ordinary newspaper buyers are not particularly tolerant and, having once tried a new paper and found it unacceptable, they were unlikely to give it a second chance. So the chance in the first week of May 1975 was lost.

But if, against all these odds, the *Scottish Daily News* had survived, what would that have proved? That a group of shop-floor workers, with professional help, could run a daily newspaper. That would only have come as a surprise to people who either have a very low opinion of the intelligence of shop-floor workers or are unfamiliar with the quality of management in some newspapers, as in some other industries. Management does not have a monopoly of virtue or of intelligence, even when it comes to managerial skills. And since the co-operative had a more or less copper-bottomed guarantee that there would be no interruptions to production and no wage demands and no working to rule, they had a considerable advantage, especially over the previous Beaverbrook management in Albion Street.

If the project had survived it would also have indicated ways in which the tension between worker-directors and professional management could have been resolved. This is certain to be an area of difficulty in any enterprise *controlled* by the workers unless, of course, the workers unquestioningly adopt the assumptions and values of professional management; it is hard to imagine that any group of workers accepting these values would also have the vision to try to control the whole operation.

Although both Allister Mackie and Eric Tough claim that the co-operative was starting to come to terms with the distinction between policy-making and day-to-day management, seemingly intractable problems remained unsolved. Any worker with a coherent, left-wing political stance is

162

bound to see a political content in many issues which a manager would regard as day-to-day business. The joke about the price of pies in the canteen is more than a joke; the question of whether a works canteen is to be subsidised or not by the company has a political content. And the matter of the editorial content of the product, in the case of a newspaper, is also politically loaded. A group of workers trying to change society by showing that a workers' co-operative can work within the capitalist system are likely to demand that their newspaper takes an editorial line on all matters which is, at least, consistent with that aim and to concentrate on topics which tend to consolidate that political stance. So that, when Eric Tough complains about the commercial unrealism displayed by those journalists who concentrated on stories with a left-wing bias — the Ladbrokes strikers, for example — he may well be missing one of the more important points of a newspaper run as a workers' co-operative.

But if a newspaper sets itself up to reflect the views of workers, to adopt a left political stance, it must at least be consistent to that audience it has identified. To run a series of committed, front page stories — on steel or Cambodia for example — alongside a lip-smacking report of a girl strangled after intercourse, with her own bra, or a fetishist convicted of stealing thousands of women's pants, shows a naïve and markedly illogical political approach. Politics, as at least some of the workers were aware, extend further than the factory or pressroom door, pervading every aspect of day-to-day life. The left-of-centre politics of the *Scottish Daily News* were sectionalised neatly into the top left of the leader and front pages, never being allowed to intrude into the features or sports pages where, it could scarcely be disputed, the examination of a football club which discriminates against Catholics, or the influence of entertainment entrepreneurs in shaping television, are intensely political and strongly interesting topics. This schizophrenic approach failed to appeal to the political reader, who resented the trivialisation of ideas and ideals, or to the apolitical, who saw the paper as weak-kneed and gauche. The much-heralded breath of fresh air blowing through its pages had turned out to be a stale draught.

The one section of the workforce which failed glaringly

was the editorial. Never perhaps in British newspaper history have journalists been given unbridled freedom to come up with exactly the kind of newspaper they believed in, written in a style to suit *them* rather than a proprietor or the notional admass reader. What was produced was a blurred stereotype, tokenly including all the ingredients, but without the panache or moral fervour of its rivals. There was a gap in the Scottish newspaper market but what was needed, for the *Daily News* to survive, was a substantial hole. And the editorial combustion generated was not sufficiently powerful to expand the niche.

Responsibility for the editorial failure must lie with editor Fred Sillitto and his executive journalists. Sillitto was clearly not up to the job; he was an old man in newspaper years and his ideas reflected his personality — low-key, accommodating, slightly obscure. The end result was simply that he did not edit. The newspaper appeared at the end of the night as a patchwork of separate, wildly clashing views, opinions and identities. A strong editor could have imprinted his vision over the columns. Sillitto was neither firm nor visionary. He had been installed in the editor's chair to keep it warm until the competitors for it completed their eliminator for the title. And when his successor, Nathan Goldberg, finally won through, the goodwill and the circulation had been squandered.

As a newspaper, then, the *Scottish Daily News* failed to match up to expectations even if, towards the end, it was starting to come together as an orthodox popular tabloid. And as a workers' co-operative it was fatally undermined by internal pressures, most of them centred on Robert Maxwell. Given these two conditions, then, should the workforce have abandoned the struggle sooner in order to avoid the indignity and ignominy of the final weeks? At various points in the downhill progress of the enterprise a small minority of workers, who saw the idea of a co-operative as more important than saving jobs at any price, seriously considered 'pulling the plugs' on the newspaper. It was the one weapon they had against Maxwell's inexorable rise to a position of control; but it was terrifying to contemplate using it. Nevertheless three union branches might have provided the idealism and the determination to kill off the monster that has grown out of their efforts — the electricians, the engineers and the clerical workers. Of the three the engineers were the likeliest to take action, being a small group of skilled craftsmen who play a critical role in the production of the newspaper. And several times during June and July as it became clear that Maxwell was not going to be dislodged by the workforce the AUEW chapel considered stopping production, in the full knowledge that one lost day would be fatal to the whole enterprise. They pulled back from the brink for two obvious reasons: they hesitated to take a decision that would impose their will on the workforce, and they retained a forlorn hope that the situation might change for the better if they gave the paper more time.

In retrospect — and from a safe distance — it is easy to say that suicide would have been a brave and honourable way out of the mess; it would at least have spared the workforce the indignities that marked the final weeks — appeals for help, recriminations, emergency editions and even collecting cans in the streets of Glasgow — and it would have proclaimed the workers' faith in themselves. But no one standing on the sidelines had the right to suggest to men and women who had already tasted the miseries of unemployment that they should consign themselves to that state again for the sake of an ideal. And certainly the majority of the workforce utterly rejected the notion of suicide, if it even occurred to them as a possibility. They had put too much of themselves and their hopes into the enterprise to face up to the reality of what had happened to it.

If ripples from the *Scottish Daily News* are still lapping around the newspaper industry, the spot where the stone first hit the water now lies still. The great, black, shiny building in Albion Street lies empty with only a few tattered remnants of what went on there. The Express Bar next door still has the 'Ex . . .' covered with the blue logo, of the *Daily News*. A few 'Save the *News*' posters still stick to the glass windows high up on the building. And 500 people still have vivid memories of an exhilarating frustrating experience. The circulation of the *Scottish Daily Express* has expanded to fill most of the gap left when the *Daily News* ceased publication (Beaverbrook ran an ill-disguised poster campaign after the closure inviting former *News* readers, 'For the *NEWS* get the *EXPRESS*') and the other Scottish.

newspapers breathed a sigh of relief that the menace to their circulation and to their established practices had gone from the scene.

The questions which the *Scottish Daily News* might have answered remain unresolved and must await the next opportunity, if there is another: for, although the crisis in the newspaper industry will continue and deepen, it is difficult to imagine that the same components will coincide again to produce another attempt by newspaper workers to take over from the bosses.

THE END

Index

168

169